SANITY IN BEDLAM:
A Study of Robert Burton's
Anatomy of Melancholy

DATE DUE FOR RETURN

SANITY IN BEDLAM:

A Study of Robert Burton's

Anatomy of Melancholy

LAWRENCE BABB

GREENWOOD PRESS, PUBLISHERS
WESTPORT, CONNECTICUT

Library of Congress Cataloging in Publication Data

Babb, Lawrence.
    Sanity in bedlam.

    Reprint of the ed. published by Michigan State Uni-
versity Press, East Lansing.
    Bibliography: p.
    Includes index.
    1. Burton, Robert, 1577-1640. The anatomy of melan-
choly. 2. Melancholy. I. Title.
[PR2224.B3 1977]   828'.3'07   77-13309
ISBN 0-8371-9856-9

Reprinted in 1977 by Greenwood Press, Inc.,
51 Riverside Avenue, Westport, CT. 06880

Printed in the United States of America

To Frances

CONTENTS

FOREWORD

THE MODERN EDITION of the *Anatomy* which I have used is that of A. R. Shilleto, 3 vols., London, 1926-27. I have referred to volume and page of the Shilleto edition in this fashion: 1.45, 3.264. For study of the seventeenth century editions, I have had access to the copies in the Henry E. Huntington Library.

I am greatly indebted to my colleagues Claude M. Newlin, George R. Price, and Arnold Williams and to Paul Jordan-Smith, the most distinguished of Burton scholars, for their reading of the manuscript and their candid and valuable criticism.

LAWRENCE BABB

East Lansing
March 27, 1959

INTRODUCTION

ROBERT BURTON's early Stuart contemporaries evidently found much pleasure and profit in his *Anatomy of Melancholy*, for they bought five editions of it during his lifetime. Its popularity waned rapidly, however, during the Commonwealth and Restoration periods. Its scientific lore was already out of date and the tautology of its style already out of vogue. The book remained in relative obscurity throughout the eighteenth century.

During the Romantic Period, there was a revival of interest, due largely to the enthusiasm of Charles Lamb and other men of letters. Forty-one editions and reissues of the *Anatomy* were published in the nineteenth century. In our own century, interest in Burton's work has continued, at least slowly, to increase. A number of appreciative essays have accumulated, and a rather limited body of Burton scholarship, some of it excellent, has developed. Also, because the book contains useful documentation on a great variety of subjects, it has been much quarried for representative quotations by scholars in various seventeenth century fields. *The Anatomy of Melancholy* has become a very familiar title. Indeed "anatomy" in its seventeenth century sense has begun to appear somewhat frequently in contemporary titles.

There remains a certain vagueness, however, about the nature and purposes of Burton's book, and its reputation is consequently less than it deserves. Most students of English literature are aware that it deals with abnormal psychology, that it is whimsical, eccentric, and charming, that it contains much wit and wisdom, and that it is one of the more important works of its period. Only the assiduous student of Burton is likely to have formed a more definite idea. For the book is very long; its content is heterogeneous and not too well ordered; its timeless elements are confusedly intermingled with the obsolete. Neither its meanings nor its merits are immediately obvious.

In the belief that readers might welcome some clarification, I am presenting a study which might be called "a preface to Burton's *Anatomy*." I have tried to define the author's aims, methods, beliefs, and accomplishments. When it seemed helpful, I have attempted to fill in the seventeenth century background. I have incorporated the findings of earlier Burton scholarship when they seemed pertinent and valid and have made contributions of my own. I hope that I have succeeded in clearing away some of the impediments to the understanding and enjoyment of a great book.

Chapter I: THE CHARACTER AND CONTENT
OF *THE ANATOMY OF
MELANCHOLY*

WHEN *The Anatomy of Melancholy* was first published in 1621, the title
would have announced to the Jacobean book buyer that this was a treatise
of analytical character in the field of psychopathology. In Renaissance
language *melancholy* is a psychiatric term denoting a morbid depression
of mind. *Anatomy* means literally "dissection," figuratively "analysis."
The word appears frequently in Renaissance titles.[1] The subtitle indicates
that the author has a lively consciousness of the literal meaning behind
the figure, for it states that the subject has been "Philosophically, Medi-
cinally, Historically, Opened and Cvt Vp."

Although he reveals his identity elsewhere, the author calls himself
"Democritus Junior" on the title page. He suggests thus a spiritual kinship
with Democritus of ancient Abdera, who was known to the Renaissance
as a melancholic eccentric, the "laughing philosopher" (see Chap. III).
The pseudonym suggests that the technical material will be seasoned with
satire.

The book was very successful. Burton's contemporary Thomas Fuller
writes that "Scarce any book of philology in our land hath in so short a
time passed so many impressions."[2] According to Anthony Wood, the
publisher "got an estate by it."[3] "The first, second, and third editions
were suddenly gone, eagerly read" (*Anatomy*, 1.27). These appeared
respectively in 1621, 1624, and 1628. The fourth edition followed in 1632.
The fifth edition, apparently delayed beyond its due time,[4] was not
published until 1638. Thereafter the demand seems to have slackened
markedly. The sixth edition, containing Burton's last additions and revisions, was published in 1651, eleven years after his death. Each new
edition of the *Anatomy* (through the sixth) was an augmentation of the
one just before it. Only two more editions of the book appeared during
the seventeenth century (1660, 1676). The ninth edition was published
in 1800.

---

[1] Burton cites four "honourable precedents," all titles of continental works, for his
use of *anatomy* (1.17). Anthony Zara's *Anatomy of Wit* (1615), he implies, has
suggested to him the division of his work into sections, members, subsections. Paul
Jordan-Smith lists nineteen Elizabethan and Jacobean "anatomies": *Bibliographia
Burtoniana* (Stanford, Cal., 1931), p. 23.
[2] *The Worthies of England*, ed. John Freeman (London, 1952), p. 321.
[3] *Athenae Oxonienses*, ed. Philip Bliss (London, 1813-20), II, 653.
[4] See Chap. II, note 9.

The success of the earlier editions was due in part to current interest in the subject matter promised by the title. Although he does not limit himself by any means to the topic announced, Burton fulfills his promise with a comprehensive and detailed treatment of the subject of melancholy in the sense in which his contemporaries understood it.

II

The seventeenth century idea of melancholy originates in Renaissance scientific theory. Since Renaissance thinkers recognize the interreaction of body and mind, *melancholy* is both a psychological and a medical term. The concept is complex and vaguely limited.[5] In Burton's title, the word refers to a mental disease, or genus of diseases, which is copiously discussed in Renaissance, medieval, and classical works on medicine ·and psychiatry along with such other maladies as madness, frenzy, hydrophobia, and epilepsy.

The usual symptoms of the disease are fear and sorrow without external cause. The degree of its intensity may vary greatly, from relative normality to a dementia characterized by intense agony of mind and fearful hallucinations.[6] There are also many odd varieties of melancholy, so many that it sometimes seems as if Renaissance psychopathology regards all mental abnormality as melancholy. Among these is a sanguine, or laughing melancholy, which manifests itself in fits of hilarity recurring periodically. Democritus' melancholy was evidently of this variety.

The immediate cause of the melancholic malady is a physical cause, the humor melancholy (or black bile), from which the disease takes its name. This is one of the four humors, or fluids, which, according to the old physiology, constitute the fluid content of the body: blood, choler, phlegm, and melancholy. Black bile is cold and dry, black, heavy, viscid, sour. Normally it is concentrated in the spleen. Since its primary qualities (coldness and dryness) are opposite to those of a living creature (heat and moisture), it is likely to be noxious. If for any reason it becomes abnormally abundant, it produces physical debilities and mental morbidities.

In addition to the natural melancholy humor, there are unnatural

[5] Elsewhere I have dealt with this subject at much greater length: *The Elizabethan Malady: A Study of Melancholia in English Literature from 1580 to 1642* (East Lansing, Mich., 1951), pp. 21-72.

The term melancholy is used to denote not only the mental illness described here but also the melancholy *complexion*, or temperament, a relatively normal and stable condition of body and mind. The melancholy temperament is not clearly distinguishable from the melancholic malady, the difference being largely a matter of degree. *Melancholy* is, in addition, the name of one of the four humors (see below).

[6] The melancholia of the old medical works is obviously not altogether fictitious, as modern psychiatrists will testify. The agreement between Burtonian and modern psychiatry, however, does not extend far.

varieties arising from the corruption of natural humors. These are responsible for some of the atypical psychiatric symptoms.[7] Blood which has suffered melancholic corruption, for example, is the cause of the laughing melancholy.

Less immediately, the melancholic malady is caused by whatever engenders a melancholic humor. The possible causes are multifarious, some physical, some psychological. The most frequent physical cause is diet. The most frequent psychological cause is strong emotion. Fear and grief are especially likely to engender melancholy. The curative methods range from blood-letting (to evacuate the noxious humor) to kindly counsel.

The melancholy man, as every Renaissance Englishman would know, is morose, taciturn, waspish, misanthropic, solitary, fond of darkness. He commonly suffers from grotesque hallucinations. He is extremely wretched and often longs for death.

The belief that the melancholy man is anti-social, miserable, and irrational is traceable to the medical system associated with the name of Galen. In the Renaissance mind it is accompanied by and modified by another concept of the melancholy character, a concept of greater dignity. The source of this is the Aristotelian *Problemata* (XXX, i). According to the Aristotelian idea of melancholy, black bile engenders unusual intellectual and artistic powers; indeed statesmen, scholars, poets, and artists are more than likely to be melancholy. The Elizabethan and early Stuart conception of the melancholy man is compounded of these two not wholly compatible elements.

The association of melancholy with genius made the malady attractive. In the sixteenth century English travellers found it very much in vogue among the Italian intellectuals and brought it home with them. An epidemic broke out in England, apparently about 1580, and continued for several decades.[8] For some time melancholy men were so numerous in London that they constituted a social type, often called the *malcontent*. Evidence concerning the melancholy attitudes, mannerisms, and pretensions is abundant in Elizabethan and early Stuart literature, especially in the drama. Many men of letters were occasionally or chronically melancholy: Sidney, Greene, Nashe, Chapman, Breton, Donne, Browne, and others.

Burton, then, offered a book on melancholy to a melancholy generation. It is hard to think of a subject which would more certainly have insured the success of a book in 1621.

The author is, to be sure, a minister, not a physician. He feels justified in publishing a book on melancholy, however, because he has studied the

---

[7] See *Elizabethan Malady*, pp. 21-22, 33-36.
[8] For a more detailed account of the epidemic of melancholy and the literary evidence of it, see *Elizabethan Malady*, pp. 73-100.

literature of the subject assiduously and because he has himself experienced the malady. He has read and written of it in the hope of relieving himself and others (see 1.18-19).

III

Thus motivated, Burton has produced a somewhat ponderous work (1301 pages in the Shilleto edition). He seems to have laid out his material in orderly fashion. The *Anatomy* is divided into three "partitions," and these are divided into "sections," the sections into "members," the members into "subsections," each division or subdivision devoted to a major or lesser aspect of melancholy or a related subject. At the opening of each partition (each volume in the Shilleto edition), there appears an elaborate statement of the various topics and subtopics in outline form. The organizational framework of the *Anatomy* is, in fact, formidably logical, complex, and comprehensive. The distribution of material in the book is not quite so logical as one might expect, but on the whole Burton follows his outlines.

In the first volume (or "partition") he deals rather exhaustively with the causes, symptoms, and prognostics of melancholy; in the second with the cure of melancholy; in the third with all aspects of two varieties of melancholy which he sees fit to deal with apart, love melancholy (lovesickness) and religious melancholy (melancholy which either by its causes or its symptoms is associated with religion).

In expounding his melancholic material, Burton shows the respect for authority which is characteristic of most medieval and of many Renaissance writers. He quotes and cites the authors whom he has consulted not merely frequently but multitudinously. His margins bristle with references; on many pages his text consists of little else than a sequence of quotations (many of them in Latin) tied together by appropriate transitions. He himself characterizes his book as a piece of cloth woven "of divers fleeces" (1.22). Possibly the first and most lasting impression that the reader receives from the *Anatomy* is its overpowering learnedness. It seems impossible that any man could have read and absorbed so many books. The multiplicity of strange, hard-angled Latinized names at first seems very forbidding.

The *Anatomy*, however, is not heavy reading. There are, to be sure, dull stretches in it—for example, the dietary and pharmaceutical directions—, but on the whole it is a very entertaining book, largely because of the animation with which it is written.

There is considerable stylistic diversity in the *Anatomy*, as the author himself points out (1.31), yet one manner is clearly more frequent and more characteristic than any other. This is a loose and informal style which gives the impression of fluent and energetic speech.[9] It abounds in pat and homely turns of phrase and seems artlessly familiar and confidential. Burton has written "with as small deliberation" as he ordinarily speaks without concerning himself with the pretentious artificialities that others affect (1.30). He has neglected niceties of expression (1.31); his book has many faults: "barbarism, *Dorick* dialect, extemporanean style, tautologies, apish imitation, a rhapsody of rags gathered together from [many authors] . . . confusedly tumbled out, without art . . . ('tis partly affected)" (1.24). Perhaps somewhat disingenuously, he asks us to believe that his book is an unstudied outpouring in which, stylistically, he has followed his various successive impulses. It is a "confused lump" like a newborn bear cub, and he has not had "time to lick it into form" (1.30).

Informality is one of the salient characteristics of Burton's style. Another is copiousness. Cold, humid air, as he expresses the idea, is "thick, cloudy, misty, foggy air, or such as comes from fens, moorish grounds, lakes . . ." (1.275). Phrases come rushing and tumbling from a brain apparently overcharged with them in lengthy and often flamboyant catalogs. He elaborates profusely. Among the symptoms of lovesickness he includes the lover's fierce determination to demonstrate his love and furnishes illustration: " 'tis an ordinary thing for these inamoratos of our times . . . to stab their arms, carouse in blood, or [to act] as that *Thessalian Thero*, that bit off his own thumb . . . to make his Corrival do as much . . . If she bid them, they will go barefoot to *Jerusalem*, to the great *Cham's* Court, to the East *Indies*, to fetch her a bird to wear in her hat . . . [They will] serve twice seven years, as *Jacob* did for *Rachel*; do as much as *Gismunda* . . . did for *Guiscardus* her true love, eat his heart when he died; or as *Artemisia* [who] drank her husband's bones beaten to powder, and so bury him in herself, and endure more torments than *Theseus* or *Paris*" (3.191). One gets the impression that the author could go on indefinitely. His memorial ranging through his very wide reading supplies him with abundant illustrative material on almost any subject. In his discourse on jealousy, for example, he consoles the cuckold for his humiliation by pointing out that many of the greatest men of history have been cuckolds and calls to mind a rather long list of illustrious instances (3.334). His book is salted with singular examples and incredible tales.

[9] According to George Williamson, Burton is consciously a Senecan stylist; that is, he chooses Senecan plainness and informality in preference to Ciceronian artifice and periodicity. He writes for the most part in the "loose" Senecan style but sometimes adopts the more incisive "clipped" Senecan manner. See *The Senecan Amble: A Study in Prose Form from Bacon to Collier* (Chicago, 1951), pp. 198-200. There are many other commentaries on Burton's style. That of William R. Mueller (*The Anatomy of Robert Burton's England*, Berkeley and Los Angeles, 1952, pp. 27-30) seems to me especially apt.

5

A strangely small proportion of the *Anatomy* is devoted specifically to medicine and psychiatry. The first volume (concerning the causes, symptoms, and prognostics of melancholy proper) begins with a "satirical" preface, Democritus Junior's address to the reader. In this the author includes, with many other things, a coy, half-revealing self-portrait, an apology for his book, an explanation of his pseudonym, a very long satiric demonstration that all the world is unreasonable, "melancholy, mad," for the purpose of emphasizing the importance of the subject, and a utopian sketch of an ideally ordered kingdom. The reader is now on page 141.

After other prefatory bits, the *Anatomy* proper opens with a somberly eloquent subsection on "Man's Excellency, Fall, Miseries, Infirmities; The causes of them" (eight pages). This is an essay in itself, readily separable from context, with obvious resemblance to the numerous earlier treatments of the same theme. In the following subsection, the author does, to be sure, get down to the business of technical instruction. But as he proceeds along the course which he has plotted out for himself through his comprehensive subject, he continually makes extended excursions into tangential fields, excursions which sometimes are more or less justified by their connection with the train of thought, which sometimes are frankly digressions. There is "A Digression of the nature of Spirits, bad Angels, or Devils, and how they cause Melancholy," twenty-five pages of curious lore illustrated by dozens of lurid tales. There is a sixty-page treatment of the passions (as causes of melancholy), written rather in the manner of the moralist than in that of the psychologist, with abundant quotation from classical philosophers and poets, from the Church Fathers, from the Bible, etc. This treatise on the passions, like the essay on man's miseries, is a composition in itself and belongs to a traditional *genre*. There is a subsection entitled "Love of Learning, or overmuch Study. With a Digression of the Misery of Scholars, and why the Muses are Melancholy" (thirty pages). In this there are brief technical observations, but most of it is devoted to the ignominy and poverty of university scholars and of the minor Anglican clergy. This is one of the more original and earnest passages of the *Anatomy*.

Early in the second volume (on the cure of melancholy) one comes upon an extended passage bearing the title "Air rectified. With a digression of the Air" (forty pages). This section should consist of advice on what to do about climates and weathers that cause or aggravate melancholy. It opens, however, with an enthusiastic imaginative sweep through many foreign lands which Burton has never actually visited except through the reading of travel literature. He sets down a long series of questions, raised in his mind by his reading, which he would settle by personal investigation if he could only fly. Is Teneriffe actually seventy-two miles high? Is

6

there really such a South American kingdom as El Dorado? Are there really Muscovites that hibernate in the winter, lying *"fast asleep . . . benumbed with cold"* until April, when *"they revive again, and go about their business"* (2.46)? Does it really rain frogs in Norway? Soon the author is in the midst of a discussion of astronomical theory in which through many pages the theories of the Ptolemaic, Copernican, and other schools criss-cross and collide. Toward the end of the section Burton at last delivers therapeutic counsel related to climate and weather with incidental comment on the salubrious situations of various country estates that he has seen.

Immediately after the section on "air" there comes "Exercise rectified of Body and Mind" (2.80 ff.). This consists, to be sure, of therapeutic advice, but it might well stand as an independent and enthusiastic composition on recreations. The writer devotes a third of it to the pleasures of study. Farther on one comes upon "A Consolatory Digression containing the Remedies of all manner of Discontents." This again is a treatise in itself, ninety-four pages long, in which, consciously following the precedent of earlier authors,[10] Burton offers comfort for a long list of human miseries and calamities. The melancholy reader presumably will be able to find among the many topics the one which fits his case, and the reading of the pertinent passage will ease his sorrow and therefore his melancholy. Is poverty the cause of his grief? "Christ himself was poor, born in a manger, and had not a house to hide his head in all his life . . . Your great Philosophers have been voluntarily poor." Riches bring much unhappiness to their possessors (2.168-69). And so Burton deals with sickness, servitude, death of friends and kinsmen, etc. This consolatory essay obviously is the issue of his studies of Plutarch, Cicero, Seneca, Boethius, the Bible, the Church Fathers, and other moralists rather than his studies of Galen and Bernard of Gordon.

The treatise on love melancholy (in vol. III) begins at some distance from its topic. Before dealing with love melancholy in particular, Burton feels impelled to discuss love in general and does so through forty-three pages. Here, among many other things, one finds a little treatise on charity (3.32-43) which, if it were longer, might be a sermon with I Corinthians 13:13 for its text. The discussion of love melancholy, when Burton finally reaches the subject, contains various imbedded compositions, for example, a richly illustrated essay on the power of beauty (3.73-99). The section on the lover's malady closes with a discourse on the "Cure of Love-Melan-

[10] John L. Lievsay, in "Robert Burton's *De Consolatione*," *South Atlantic Quarterly*, LV (1956), 329-36, supplies the background for this part of the *Anatomy* by outlining the history of the *consolatio* and explaining its traditional pattern. Benjamin Boyce's "The Stoic *Consolatio* and Shakespeare," *Publications of the Modern Language Association*, LXIV (1949), 771-80, includes similar material and lists several English consolations of the sixteenth and seventeenth centuries.

choly" (3.218 ff.), which belongs to a traditional type. Examples in English are Lyly's "A cooling Carde for Philautus and all fond louers," appended to *Euphues*, Beaumont's *Remedy of Love*, and Sir Thomas Overbury's *Remedy of Love*. Burton cites authorities who have written on the cure of love (3.295), including Ovid, whose *Remedio Amoris* is the prototype of the *genre*. Burton's remedy of love, however, includes a very un-Ovidian feature, an extended essay on marriage (3.263-94), which he considers the happiest and most effective remedy for lovesickness.

Next comes a section on jealousy, which Burton considers a "bastard-branch, or kind of Love-Melancholy" (3.295). This has some kinship perhaps with Benedetto Varchi's *Blazon of Jealousy* (1560), which Burton seems to have known through Robert Tofte's translation of 1615. The essay on jealousy contains very few medical or psychological technicalities[11] but a great deal of description, comment, and counsel. It includes some of Burton's liveliest writing.

Very early in the treatise on religious melancholy (the last major topic in the *Anatomy*), one comes upon a discourse concerning the beauty of God and the love which it inspires (3.360-65). If it were not so brief, this might be a sermon on Psalms 27:4. As he proceeds, the author writes upon a great variety of religious topics, occasionally in such a fashion as to produce a separable composition, for instance a tirade against disbelief in its various forms (3.434-49). The *Anatomy* closes with a treatise of comfortable counsel for those with afflicted conscience (3.468-94), which appeared first in the second edition. Burton says that he wrote it at the urging of his brother George and of a former chamber-fellow in Christ Church College. Here again is a composition which belongs to a *genre* familiar to Burton's contemporaries. Burton names examples (3.468). Imbedded within it is an argument on predestination (3.479-85).

I have listed a few, but by no means all, of the separable compositions included in the *Anatomy*. Some of these are definitely assignable to recognizable literary types: the utopia, the essay on man's misery, the treatise of the passions, the comfort for the various miseries of mankind, the remedy of love, the comfort for the afflicted conscience. There are also some very sermon-like discourses in the book. Other distinguishable compositions, such as the essay on the melancholy of scholars and the "Digression of the Air," are original and personal. When one notes the presence of these various interior units, he begins to see *The Anatomy of Melancholy* as a compound book, not one work but several, the lesser discourses imbedded in the text of the greater. Besides the *Anatomy*, we have no other work by Burton except his not very impressive Latin comedy *Philosophaster* and a few Latin poems (see Chap. III, sec. i). He is really

---

[11] In writing on this subject, Burton had no large body of medical or psychiatric theory to draw on. See *Elizabethan Malady*, pp. 140-42.

a one-book author. One must remember, however, the compound character of the *Anatomy*. It might suitably be entitled *Opera Burtoni*.

The presence of the separable discourses dilutes the scientific and technical matter of the *Anatomy* considerably. The sum of the pages in these, however, would by no means indicate the extent of the dilution. For throughout the book, even in those parts which are definitely on the primary subject, the familiar essayist is continually taking over from the medical writer in a fashion too subtle to be shown by stating the content of extended homogeneous parts. In the volume on the cure of melancholy, for example, Burton comes to the subject of music. Music is among the curative measures which physicians recommend to melancholy patients for specific physiological reasons. Burton is less interested in medical reasoning, however, than simply in the pleasures of music. In his judgment, there is no means "to exhilarate a sorrowful heart . . . so present, none so powerful, none so apposite, as a cup of strong drink, mirth, musick, and merry company" (2.132). There follows a heartfelt praise of music, qualified by a warning against immoderate and frivolous indulgence, which spills over into the following subsection on "Mirth and merry company, fair objects [as] remedies" (2.137). Here the author recommends especially looking at beautiful young women, citing the experience of Epicurus as confirmation. The third volume of the *Anatomy* exhibits this kind of non-technical dilution even more strikingly than the first two. In describing love melancholy, Burton expatiates exuberantly, and in reviewing religious abominations, he is indignantly tautological.

It is quite impossible to establish a definite figure for the dilution, but one may guess. I should estimate that less than a fourth of the *Anatomy* is devoted, in any strict sense, to medicine, physiology, psychology, and psychiatry.[12]

One gets the impression that Burton, through indefatigable reading, has absorbed almost everything that his cultural milieu has to offer and that he has retained it with an unusually tenacious memory. Most of what he has absorbed he seems to have fitted into his book in one way or another. Any subject of general interest among cultivated Jacobeans is likely to turn up somewhere in the *Anatomy*, perhaps discussed at length, perhaps only mentioned. One reads of alchemy, Rosicrucianism, comets, the mines of the New World, aphrodisiacs, heraldry, botanical gardens, magnetism, chiromancy, Queen Elizabeth, Socinianism, Helen of Troy, the misanthropy of Timon of Athens, falconry, tobacco, the evanescence of

---

[12] "The writer's temperament, matched with his theme, exhibits him not merely as the physician of body and soul, but as a satirist, a humanist and a social and political reformer. . . . The general literary aspect of *The Anatomy* has so far overpowered the medical that Fuller could speak of it as a 'book of philology.' "—Edward Bensly, "Robert Burton, John Barclay and John Owen," *Cambridge History of English Literature*, IV (1910) p. 282.

beauty, the delays of the law and the venality of lawyers, amulets, simony, the vicissitudes of fortune, the decay of the world, Arminianism, Mark Anthony and Cleopatra, miraculous cures, the sin of curiosity, *praestigiae daemonum*, sycophancy in princes' courts, the machinations of the Jesuits, etc., etc.

There are, of course, omissions. Some of these suggest Burton's isolation from the life of London and the court. There is no mention of Parliamentary strife, of Sir Thomas Overbury, of the London playhouses, of festivities at court. Others are not so easily accounted for. Burton's thinking on the subject of education seems strangely deficient. One finds a great deal in his book about universities and about scholars and their interests but no serious discussion of curriculum at any educational level or of the methods or purposes of education. There is no discussion in the *Anatomy* of the gentlemanly or courtly character. Burton quotes Castiglione ("Balthasar Castilio") fairly frequently but seems to have been indifferent to the central theme of *The Courtier*. He is an assiduous user of the Bible, yet he shows no interest in the new methods of exegesis. His ideas in the field of literary criticism are few and simple (see Chap. IV, sec. ii). Although these subjects were widely discussed in Elizabethan and early Stuart England, as they were throughout western Europe, Burton seems to have given them little thought. He is indifferent, however, to very few of the interests of his contemporaries.

Because the book is so inclusive and so various and because the author's mind is absorptive rather than venturesome and original, scholars of our time have found the *Anatomy* a valuable source for quotations to represent seventeenth century ideas concerning physiology and psychology, cosmology, demonology, ethics, and other subjects. There is probably no other work which exhibits more completely the interests, acquirements, and opinions of the early Stuart intellectuals. One of the values of the *Anatomy*, though not its greatest, lies in its representative character. Every student of early Stuart England should know the book well.

IV

If Burton modelled his book on any earlier work or *genre*, it should not be hard to identify it from his own statements. He is very candid about his sources. Furthermore he is one of the many Renaissance writers in whom the intellectual diffidence of the Middle Ages persists. He is more at ease when he is resting on authority and precedent than when he is engaged in something novel. He would not be likely to pretend originality. But he does not reveal any prototype.

Scholars have been understandably hesitant about suggesting precedents. Timothy Bright's *Treatise of Melancholie* (1586)[13] is the only work

[13] Reprinted by the Facsimile Text Society, New York, 1940.

which has been seriously proposed as Burton's model. The argument supporting this proposal consists of pointing out the likenesses between Bright's chapter headings and certain section headings in the *Anatomy*.[14] It is natural, however, that two works on the same subject should deal with the same topics. Beyond some inevitable coincidence of subject matter, there is little resemblance between Bright's treatise and Burton's much more comprehensive and spirited book. Bright seems to have no special authority in Burton's mind, for his references to Bright's *Treatise* are not numerous. He refers much more often, for example, to André du Laurens' essay on melancholy.[15]

It might seem worthwhile to look among the numerous "anatomies" of the Renaissance period[16] for the model which Burton followed. But no one has proposed any of these. None of them is on the subject of melancholy, none bears any close resemblance to Burton's work, and Burton gives little evidence of acquaintanceship with them. He attributes features of his formal organization, to be sure, to the suggestion of Zara's *Anatomy of Wit* (1.17).[17]

Because of the great variety of information in the *Anatomy*, it is natural to associate it with the *compendia*, medieval and Renaissance.[18] Burton knows two of the medieval encyclopedias, Vincent of Beauvais' *Speculum Naturale* and Bartholomaeus Anglicus' *De Rerum Varietate*. He refers twice to each of these. He occasionally cites Renaissance works which might be considered encyclopedic, for example Cardan's *De Subtilitate* and *De Rerum Varietate* and Zara's *Anatomia Ingeniorum*. (He shows no knowledge of Pierre de la Primaudaye's *French Academie*, probably the most systematic and inclusive of the Renaissance works of general information.) But the *Anatomy* resembles the *compendia* merely in its comprehensiveness and in the formality of its general organization. Like the encyclopedists, Burton is one of the transmitters ("the last of the great transmitters"[19]), but the *Anatomy* obviously does not follow the encyclopedic pattern.

[14] See Paul Jordan-Smith, *Bibliographia Burtoniana*, pp. 63-65; William J. Carlton, *Timothe Bright Doctor of Phisicke* (London, 1911), pp. 51-55. Jordan-Smith names and disposes of some "Apochryphal Sources" (pp. 50-59).

[15] This is one of Burton's principal sources. It appeared first in 1597 as a part of a popular medical work by Du Laurens in French. An English translation of this by Richard Surphlet was published in London in 1599: *A Discourse of the Preservation of the Sight: of Melancholike Diseases; of Rheumes, and of Old Age* (Shakespeare Association facsimiles, No. 15, 1938). A Latin translation of the section on melancholy by Thomas Moundeford was also published in 1599 (*De Morbis Melancholicis Tractatus*). Burton uses a Latin version.

[16] See above, note 1.

[17] For information concerning this book and its diversified content, see Paul Jordan-Smith's and Floyd Dell's edition of the *Anatomy* (New York, 1928), p. 1033.

[18] See Jordan-Smith, *Bibliographia Burtoniana*, pp. 27-28.

[19] Sir William Osler, "Extract from Creators, Transmuters, and Transmitters," *Oxford Bibliographical Society Proceedings and Papers*, I (1926-27), 216.

Burton probably had no feeling that he had produced anything very singular. The early Stuart reader, moreover, would probably not have considered the *Anatomy* a particularly novel book. Two earlier treatises on melancholy were available to him in his own language, Bright's and Du Laurens'; he had seen many "anatomies"; he was quite accustomed to comprehensive and miscellaneously informative works. He would have seen a resemblance, moreover, between the *Anatomy* and the moralistic psychologies, the treatises on the passions, which by 1621 were fairly numerous (see Chap. V, sec. vi). If it is classifiable at all, the *Anatomy* belongs to this *genre*. Yet it is more limited in its announced subject, much more inclusive in its actual content, and much more animated and personal in its manner than any of these psychological treatises.

At the time of its publication, the *Anatomy* was something new, something highly individual and unpremeditatedly original. Its influence appears in occasional later works,[20] but it is still the only book of its kind.

[20] For information on the influence of the *Anatomy* and on the history of its critical reputation, see Jordan-Smith, *Bibliographia Burtoniana*, pp. 103-09; Mueller, *Anatomy of Burton's England*, pp. 1-7. Robert G. Hallwachs' unpublished master's thesis, *The Vogue of Robert Burton, 1798-1832* (Illinois, 1937), deals more intensively with a limited period. Hallwachs finds that the publication in 1798 of John Ferriar's *Illustrations of Sterne*, which reveals Sterne's unacknowledged borrowings from the *Anatomy*, was the immediate impetus which started the Burton revival of the Romantic Period. Lamb and Keats were the Romantic writers most influenced by Burton. Robert Gittings (*John Keats: The Living Year*, Cambridge, Mass., 1954, pp. 215-23 *et passim*) reviews Keats' use of the *Anatomy*.

Burton's influence on the drama of John Ford has been much discussed by modern scholars and, I think, greatly exaggerated. See, for example, Robert Devril, *Le Drame de John Ford* (Paris, 1954), pp. 187-233. Burton's "Abstract of Melancholy" (*Anatomy*, 1.9-10) has been several times proposed as the inspiration of Milton's "L'Allegro" and "Il Penseroso." This seems to me a very questionable proposal (see Lawrence Babb. "The Background of 'Il Penseroso,'" *Studies in Philology*, XXXVII [1940], 272-73).

Charles Lamb wrote an imitation of Burton's style: *Curious Fragments, Extracted from a Common-place Book, Which Belonged to Robert Burton* (see *The Works of Charles and Mary Lamb*, ed. Thomas Hutchinson, London, 1924, I, 37-43; II, 551-52). In *The Anatomy of Bibliomania* (London, 1932), Holbrook Jackson adopts Burton's manner and methods of composition and often echoes his phraseology.

Chapter II: GENESIS AND DEVELOPMENT

BURTON's study of melancholy and his writing of the *Anatomy* were motivated by his own real or supposed illness. He first undertook the task, he says, to ease his mind, "for I had *gravidum cor, foedum caput,* a kind of imposthume in my head ... Besides I might not well refrain, for *ubi dolor, ibi digitus,* one must needs scratch where it itches ... To do myself good I turned over such physicians as our Libraries would afford, or my private friends impart" (1.18-19). By his labors he hoped not only to gain the knowledge required for self-treatment but also to avoid idleness, than which there is "no greater cause of melancholy" (1.17). He does not claim to have cured himself, but it is evident that he found the study of melancholy a diverting and an engrossing occupation which might indeed have had therapeutic value.

Burton hoped, furthermore, to serve other melancholiacs, for whom he had "a fellow-feeling" (1.19). He has written "that every man that is in any measure affected with this malady, may know how to examine it in himself, and apply remedies unto it" (1.200; *cf.* 1.37, 159).

He says little about how and when his book took form. At some unspecified time before 1620, this melancholy patient decided to investigate the disease for himself, to acquire the technical knowledge which would enable him to see himself objectively, and to take steps toward remedy. Possibly a collection of notes (he refers to a "confused company of notes," 1.30) began to take the form of a treatise, and the idea of offering this to other patients for their aid and comfort would then occur to him.

Having embarked upon the study of psychiatry, Burton evidently found it fascinating, so much so that his more proper studies in humanity and divinity suffered: "I was ... carried away by this by-stream, which, as a rillet, is deducted from the main channel of my studies" (1.34). He promises that he "will hereafter make ... amends in some treatise of divinity" (1.37), but no such treatise exists.

It may be that Burton suffered a long and severe illness between his sixteenth and twenty-second years.[1] There is, to be sure, no evidence for this beyond the fact that there appears to have been a long interruption of his undergraduate studies at Oxford. Such an illness could leave permanent effects in a sensitive and introspective mind. Burton might have been melancholically disposed from his early twenties on. He might therefore have begun his melancholic studies rather early in life. He

[1] This is the conjecture of Arthur W. Fox in "The Humorist: Robert Burton," *A Book of Bachelors* (Westminister, 1899), pp. 400-01 (note).

13

was forty-three years old when he signed the postscript to the first edition of the *Anatomy* on December 5, 1620. He might already have spent twenty years in the study of his subject and in piecing his book together. The fact that he has followed the example of Zara's *Anatomy of Wit* in dividing his book into sections, members, and subsections possibly means that he did not finally organize his book until after 1615, when Zara's book was published. But it may mean merely that he has borrowed terminology from Zara.

There is no reason to suppose that Burton intended anything more than a psychiatric treatise when he began shaping notes into a book, anything more than a treatise with perhaps such elegant ornament and such brief digressions as are found in Bright's and Du Laurens' treatises on melancholy. But as he set down the causes of melancholy, the list would have grown very long and would have carried him far from physiology and formal psychology. It would have included personal misfortunes, failures, and griefs; greed, ambition, envy, hatred, fear, and the other passions which worry and toss the souls of men; the social dislocations and injustices which bring unmerited suffering into many individual lives. Burton would have discovered that, to write comprehensively of the causes of melancholy, he would have to cover the sins, errors, and tribulations of mankind.

In enumerating the causes of melancholy, moreover, it would have occurred to him that they spare no one. Every man suffers psychological injury from sin and folly, his own and other men's. Melancholy therefore is universal: "all the world is mad . . . is melancholy, dotes. . . . who is not a fool? Who is free from melancholy? . . . In whom doth not passion, anger, envy, discontent, fear, and sorrow, reign? Who labours not of this disease?" (1.38-39). Take "melancholy in what sense you will . . . truly, or metaphorically, 'tis all one" (1.40).

He would soon have perceived that, in writing of the cure of melancholy, he could not stop with pharmaceutical, surgical, and dietary remedies. Purely medical therapy would not touch the basic psychological and social causes of the melancholy of mankind. He therefore offers counsel for the individual man on the conduct of his life, both subjective and social, and plans a thorough reordering of human society according to rational principles.

Thus psychiatry becomes the secondary theme, the conditions of human life the primary theme.[2] The length and comprehensiveness of the

[2] "No book was ever so belied by its title as the *Anatomy of Melancholy*. In reality [it is] the anatomy of man . . ." Sir William Osler, "Creators, Transmuters, and Transmitters," p. 217; the *Anatomy* is "a commentary upon the life and habits of the human race," Holbrook Jackson, *Book-Collector's Quarterly*, No. I (1930-31), p. 13; "the remedy for melancholy . . . is another name for the secret of happiness," John Middleton Murry, "Burton's 'Anatomy,'" *Countries of the Mind* (London,

Anatomy are partly due to the author's natural digressiveness and his love of collecting curiosities. Its size and scope are due in greater part, however, to his interest in the human ramifications of the technical subject. The book which Burton finally produced is devoted primarily to the representation and analysis of mankind's self-created predicament and to remedial suggestions.

The *Anatomy* must have absorbed much of Burton's energies over a period of years. As its scope increased, he would see less and less reason to lay it aside to write anything else. He could easily make a place in it for an essay on any subject which he might feel moved to treat. Anything of value which he found in his reading—interesting or pertinent information, significant opinion, apt or beautiful phrasing of an idea—could be inserted somewhere as elaboration or ornament. There was no need for the author of the *Anatomy* to write another book.

As he applied himself to representing mankind's inhumanity to man, he would develop confidence in his satiric talent, and this confidence would suggest to him the role of Democritus Junior, a role clearly appropriate both to the subject and to the style of the book. The choice of the pseudonym and the writing of the satirical preface probably did not occur until the *Anatomy* of 1621 was near completion. Burton plays his role of Democritus Junior in the preface, not in the body of the book.[3]

II

The composition of the *Anatomy* continued for nearly twenty years after its initial publication. The length of the first edition (excluding the marginalia and the minor introductory pieces) is between 300,000 and 310,000 words. The length of the sixth is between 480,000 and 490,000 words, an increase of about sixty per cent. The greatest enlargement occurs between the first and second editions. Thereafter the rate of growth becomes progressively slower. The increase of the sixth edition over the fifth is slight.

The first edition of the *Anatomy* is a somewhat thick quarto volume.[4] It lacks several of the prefatory features appearing in modern reprints, and the opening consequently seems pleasantly uncluttered. There is a type-set title page followed by a one-page dedication to Lord Berkeley. Then comes "Democritus Junior to the Reader" (seventy-two pages). The short prose passage addressed to "Lectori Male Feriato" follows

---

1931), p. 47; Burton's "subject is the soul, body, and whole life of man, and he writes both as a divine and a physician," Douglas Bush, *English Literature in the Earlier Seventeenth Century* (Oxford, 1945), p. 282.

[3] The only occurence of "Democritus Junior" which I have found in the body of the *Anatomy* (Shilleto, 1.363) was added in the fifth edition.

[4] Paul Jordan-Smith gives detailed bibliographical information on the various seventeenth century editions: *Bibliographia Burtoniana*, pp. 80-92.

(lacking the Latin verses appended to it in later editions). At the beginning of each of the three partitions, one finds, as in all later editions, an outline, or "synopsis," of its content. The book closes with a six-page postscript, to which Burton signs his name.

Although the volume is considerably briefer than the later editions, it is substantially the book that modern readers know. A comparison of the synopses in the sixth edition with those in the first reveals (aside from minor verbal variations) only one change: a single topic, "Symptoms of Maids', Nuns', and Widows' Melancholy," has been added.[5] With this one exception, then, every topic and subtopic treated in the last edition is treated in the first. The arrangement is identical. Even the titles of the various divisions are virtually the same in all editions.

It may be that, when his first edition was published, Burton regarded this as the final form of the *Anatomy*. If so, the idea of a second and enlarged edition occurred to him soon (encouraged perhaps by the success of the book), for evidently he did not remain idle for long. During the three-year interval between the first two editions, he enlarged his treatise by nearly a fourth.

The second edition (1624) is a folio (as are all subsequent seventeenth century editions). The author has dropped the postscript. This is the only unit which he ever cut out of his book. He did not, however, simply throw it away, for he used about three-fifths of it elsewhere in the second and later editions. Most of the transferred material[6] appears in the early part of the satirical preface. He has greatly lengthened the final subsection on the cure of religious despair (very brief in the first edition) by adding to it his comfort for the distressed conscience, written at the urging of his brother George and a quondam Oxford chamber-fellow. This passage (twenty-seven pages) is the only substantial continuous addition which Burton made to the *Anatomy* after its initial publication.[7] An index—not a very helpful one—appears at the close (the index is a feature also of later editions).

In the third edition (1628) the type-set title page is replaced by the

[5] See Shilleto, 1.476. The new subsection appears first in the third edition.

[6] More than three-quarters of it appears in the Shilleto edition on pages 1.24-33. At this point Burton expands twenty-one lines of the original preface to 171 lines in the second edition. The transferred material does not appear continuously or in its original order, but there is not much phraseological change in it. With the second edition this passage settles down to the comparative stability which is characteristic of the *Anatomy*. Other transferred material appears in the last paragraph of the general preface (Shilleto, 1.140-41) and in the preface to the sections on love melancholy (3.8-9).

[7] The subsection on women's melancholies, added in the third edition, is rather brief (three and one-half folio pages in its earliest form). The passage in the preface discussed in the preceding note is, of course, greatly expanded in the second edition. About two-fifths of the expansion, however, consists of material from the discarded postscript.

familiar engraved title page, which, in addition to the name of the book and the author's pseudonym, displays pictures of Democritus of Abdera, four melancholic types, the author himself, and lesser items.[8] There are two other new prefatory embellishments, the Latin verses entitled "Democritus Junior ad Librum Suum" and the English verses entitled "The Author's Abstract of Melancholy." In the body of the work, Burton inserts the subsection on "Symptoms of Maids', Nuns', and Widows' Melancholy" (Shilleto, 1.476-81), inspired apparently by a recent reading of treatises on women's ailments by Lodovicus Mercatus and Rodericus a Castro.

In the preface of the third edition, Burton declares that he is "now resolued neuer to put this Treatise out again, *Ne quid nimis*, I will not hereafter add, alter, or retract, I haue done" (*cf.* Shilleto, 1.33). But he has not done, for there is a fourth edition with further augmentation. In this the doggerel "Argument of the Frontispiece" appears for the first time. Ten lines of Latin verse are added to "Lectori Male Feriato." The *Anatomy* has now reached virtually the form in which it is generally known.

Burton asserts once more, in the preface to the fourth edition, that he will labor no more on his book. Yet there is a fifth edition, published in 1638. Evidently publication had been delayed by complications arising from an attempted piracy.[9] In the preface of this, Burton declares for the third time that he has "done." He survived the publication of this edition by only two years, but in these two years he continued to tinker with his book. The final light touches which he gave it are included in the sixth edition (1651). The publisher, Henry Cripps, explains in a postscript that the author left with him a copy of the book "exactly corrected, with severall considerable Additions by his own hand . . . with directions to have those Additions inserted in the next Edition." He has, he says, faithfully carried out the author's injunction. The sixth edition is not noticeably more correct than the earlier ones.

[8] See William R. Mueller, "Robert Burton's Frontispiece," *Publications of the Modern Language Association*, LXIV (1949), 1074-88, for discussion of the various features of the engraved title page and their meanings. On the title page of the fifth and later editions, Burton wears a skull cap.

[9] Part of the fifth edition was printed in Edinburgh, part in London, and part in Oxford. Robert Young, the would-be pirate, began the printing of the book in his Edinburgh establishment. Apparently he was stopped by Henry Cripps of Oxford, the publisher of the first seven editions of the *Anatomy*. Cripps gained possession of the sheets which Young had printed. The printing was completed in London and Oxford, and the book was assembled in Oxford and issued by Cripps. See E. Gordon Duff, "The Fifth Edition of Burton's *Anatomy of Melancholy*," *Library*, 4th series, IV (1923-24), 81-101. At the close of the volume Burton appends a Latin note expressing his irritation with the quarrelsome printers. Yet Burton himself may have been responsible to some extent for their altercations. Duff's evidence indicates that he was co-operating with Young before Cripps learned what was happening.

III

The text of the *Anatomy* expands, at a diminishing rate, until the book is more than half again as long as it was originally. The added material is not distributed evenly through the book. The satirical preface is seventy per cent longer in the sixth edition than in the first. The passage on the recreational value of study (Shilleto, 2.100-12) and certain parts of the section on love melancholy have more than doubled. On the other hand, the first section of the *Anatomy* proper (Shilleto, 1.149-202) is very little expanded. Except for the essay on man's excellency and misery, the twenty subsections included in this are devoted to such technical subjects as anatomy, psychology, and psychiatry. Burton tends to add much more generously to the non-technical passages of the *Anatomy* than to those concerned with medicine and psychology.[10]

To show how the *Anatomy* grew, I shall review the successive versions of six representative selections.[11] I shall consider first the initial fourteen pages of the satirical preface (Shilleto, 1.11-24), devoted principally to the author's comments on his pseudonym, on his way of life, and on the character of his book. In the first edition the passage consists of about 3400 words.

It is about 950 words longer in the second edition, an increase of twenty-eight per cent. To elaborate on ideas already present in the first version, the author has inserted quotations from or citations of Lucian, Erasmus, Thucydides, Synesius, Horace, Pliny, Strada, Lucretius, Varro, Aelian, Isocrates. He has returned to J. C. Scaliger's *Exercitationes* to augment material from it which he had used in the first edition. He has added about thirty lines to say that, in his isolation from the world, he looks

[10] Robert G. Hallwachs provides statistical evidence of this in his unpublished dissertation, "Additions and Revisions in the Second Edition of Burton's *Anatomy of Melancholy*" (Princeton, 1934). He finds that, in the expansions of 1624, Burton neglects technical subjects in favor of love, "curious lore," and religious, moral, and social questions (pp. 110-20).

[11] Two other parts of the *Anatomy* have had similar treatment. J. Max Patrick's article, "Robert Burton's Utopianism," *Philological Quarterly*, XXVII (1948), 345-58, includes a study of the development through the various editions of Burton's sketch of an ideal commonwealth (Shilleto, 1.109-22). This passage, Patrick finds, increases to almost three times its original length; references to additional books in successive versions indicate that Burton continued his reading; the basic ideas remain the same. Robert M. Browne in "Robert Burton and the New Cosmology," *Modern Language Quarterly*, XIII (1952), 131-48, compares the successive versions of the "Digression of the Air" (2.40-80). He notes an increase in length of fifty percent (p. 131), shows that after 1621 Burton read several new authors and picked up several new cosmological ideas which interested him, but finds no fundamental change of opinion or attitude.

Hallwachs has compared the first and second editions in their entirety. He finds "no evidence to show that [Burton's] attitude toward his book, or his fundamental ideas and opinions in general change in any significant way between 1621 and 1624" (p. 170).

upon its turmoils with amused detachment as if from a height. In developing this idea he borrows from Heinsius and Cyprian.

In the third edition the passage has again increased considerably in length, this time by about 650 words (nineteen per cent of the original length). There are two instances of basic revision: Burton has rewritten his reference to his confined academic life and expanded it to include praise of Oxford and its libraries (Shilleto, 1.13-14). He has cut a complaint concerning his failure to get preferment (Shilleto, 1.14) from fifty-two words to nineteen, with the result that it hardly seems a complaint any longer. This is the only instance of significant reduction in the passages which I have chosen for examination. Most of the increase in the third edition is accounted for by numerous and scattered minor additions. Authors newly cited include Jovius, Palingenius, Jerome, Martial.

The passage is sixty-six words longer in the fourth edition. Burton adds some detail concerning his isolation from the turmoils of the world (Shilleto, 1.15-16), slightly expands his defense of his practice of citing his sources (Shilleto, 1.23), and makes various minor insertions. There is little change in the fifth and sixth editions. In these, twenty-six words are added to the author's self-characterization as the remote spectator, and there are some very minor alterations.

The passage has grown, at a rate which diminishes rapidly through the successive editions, until it has become about fifty per cent longer than it was in the first edition. It has not, however, become essentially different. Burton's representation of himself as the detached and critical spectator, which appears first in the second edition, is the only new thought.

Next I shall examine the subsection "Of Witches and Magicians, how they cause Melancholy" (Shilleto, 1.230-34). This is actually devoted not so much to witches' and magicians' engendering of melancholy as to their wicked practices in general. The first version consists of about eighteen hundred words. In the second edition it has been expanded by about eight hundred words. The author has inserted three new items in his enumeration of witches' sinister powers and activities: they can tell men where their absent friends are and what they are doing, they can transport men's "*sweet hearts to them by night, vpon a Goats backe flying in the ayre*," they "*steale young children out of their cradles*," substituting changelings. The last two of these he has taken from Sigismundus Scherertzius' *Libellus Consolatorius de Spectris* (1621). He also adds Hercules de Saxonia to the authorities cited.

In the third edition, he adds only a few words and refers to only one new authority, Johann Nider. The subsection is considerably expanded, however, in the fourth edition, principally by hair-raising instances drawn from Jean Jacques Boissard's *De Divinatione et Magicis*

Praestigiis (?1615). Burton inserts also new material from or references to seven other books. New items of information appear: great men's reprehensible traffic with witches, witches' ability to confer insensibility to pain, the trivial nature of the activities of the "vulgar sort" of witches. The additions amount to about seven hundred words. Changes in the fifth and sixth editions are negligible.

The final version is nearly twice as long as the original. The effect of the additions, most of them appearing first in the fourth edition, has been to make the unit somewhat more informative (or misinformative) and much more specific and colorful.

"Symptoms or Signs [of melancholy] in the Mind" (Shilleto, 1.442-56) consists, in the first edition, of about 3300 words. In the second edition it has been enlarged by about five hundred words. More than a third of these are devoted to qualifying an idea stated in the first edition, the Hippocratic principle that fear and sorrow are invariable symptoms of melancholy (*Aphorisms*, VI, xxiii). Burton cites two ancients, Diocles and Aristotle, and two "*Iuniors*," Hercules de Saxonia and Baptista Porta, who believe that there are exceptions to this rule. He concludes that melancholy men "are not always sad & fearefull, but vsually so." The qualifying insertion is made without alteration of the immediate context. In other parts of the subsection, Burton inserts statements from or paraphrases of Jason Pratensis (on melancholy despair of salvation), Lord Howard (on the virtue of melancholy in the fostering of wit), Hercules de Saxonia again (on the fearless recklessness of some melancholics), Frambesarius (on the absurd imaginings of melancholics and on their taciturnity). Although these quotations and citations are new, the ideas that they support appear in the original version. There are other minor additions.

In the third edition the unit is even more extensively expanded, this time by about eleven hundred words. Burton adds references to four Renaissance physicians (Lodovicus Mercatus, Rodericus a Fonseca, Mercurialis, and Felix Plater), he inserts tales from Suetonius and Vives, and he quotes from Horace and Persius. Most of the new material, however, consists of elaboration and illustration of his own. No new ideas appear.

In the fourth edition the subsection is only about 250 words longer than in the third. The additions include Burton's sole reference to Dürer's engraving *Melencolia*. Only minor insertions appear in the fifth and sixth editions.

In the course of its development, "Symptoms . . . in the Mind" has increased by about fifty-seven per cent. The qualification of the Hippocratic aphorism is the only new idea. The subsection has gained through the addition of much specific illustration and some happy stylistic touches. On the whole, however, one has the feeling that, in the process of expansion, fluency has become verbosity.

The notable feature of the successive enlargements of "Diet rectified in Substance" (Shilleto, 2.24-30) is a disproportion. Nearly all of the insertions concern water. Burton has very little to add to his initial treatment of other items of diet, but in each new version he introduces new information on the qualities which distinguish good drinking water or on the methods by which water is obtained, transported, and stored (eight lines of it in the second edition, two in the third, fourteen in the fourth, eleven in the fifth, six in the sixth). Evidently this is a subject of persistent interest and concern to him. (He is *"aquae potor,"* drinks "no wine at all," 1.30.) Much of the new material comes from books about foreign lands. The subsection increases from about fifteen hundred words to about twenty-one hundred (forty per cent), the greatest increase occurring in the fourth edition.

"Prognosticks of Love-Melancholy" (Shilleto, 3.212-17), which deals with the prodigious results of the lover's malady, consists in the first edition of about twelve hundred words. The author refers to medical authorities, quotes from literary and pious works, and tells illustrative tales. In the second edition the unit is about four hundred words longer. The increase is largely due to the insertion of new verse quotations: from Buchanan (*Sylvae*), Virgil (*Eclogues* and *Aeneid*), Calcagninus, Anacreon, Ovid (*Metamorphoses*), and most notably Shakespeare (the final couplet of *Romeo and Juliet*). There are some new tales of the astonishing deportment of lovers, for example the story of Gismunda. No additional physicians are cited.

The author's interest in the prognosis of love seems to have waned after 1624, for the passage is little expanded in subsequent versions. Quotations from Theodorus Prodromus' romance, *The Story of Rhodanthe and Dosicles*, and from Sallust appear in the third edition. In the fourth edition Burton adds references to Parthenius' *Erotica* and Plutarch's *Amatoriae Narrationes* and tells the story of Medea's destruction of her little brother for the sake of her lover. There are no meaningful changes at all in the fifth and sixth editions.

The added material in this subsection, although it increases its length by about forty per cent, serves merely as additional embellishment of a text already somewhat embellished.

"Symptoms of Jealousy" (Shilleto, 3.321-29) consists mainly of a very spirited account of the unreasonable behavior of jealous men and women but includes also material concerning tests for virginity and national customs (mostly Levantine) arising from male jealousy. The first version of it runs to about two thousand words. Successive expansions increase its length by about forty-three percent. Nothing really new is added, but no reader would prefer brevity to the verve of the additions.

I shall reproduce a passage from this section (*cf.* Shilleto, 3.321-23) in such a fashion as to show the successive layers of accretion. The following is transcribed from the third edition. The original version is in Roman type; material which appeared first in the second edition is in italics; material which appeared first in the third edition is in small capitals; later insertions are bracketed. I cannot, obviously, reproduce Burton's italicization, and I have omitted the marginal notes.

'Tis a more vehement passion, a more furious perturbation, a bitter paine, a fire, A PERNITIOUS CURIOSITY, A GAULE CORRUPTING THE HONY OF OUR LIFE, madnesse, [vertigo,] plague, hell: They are more then ordinarily disquieted, [they loose bonum pacis, as Chrysostome obserues, and though they bee rich, keepe sumptuous tables, be nobly allied, yet miserimi omnium sunt, they are most miserable: they are more then ordinarily discontent, more sad, nihil tristius,][12] more then ordinarily[13] suspitious. Jealousie, saith Vives, begets vnquietnes in the mind, night and day: he hunts after every word he heares, every whisper, and amplifies it to himselfe *(as all melancholy men doe in other matters)* with a most iniust calumny of others, he misinterprets every thing is said or done, most apt to mistake and[14] misconster, he pryes in[15] every corner, followes close, obserues to an haire. *'Tis proper to Iealousie so to doe,*

> *Pale hag, infernall fury, pleasures smart,*
> *Envies obseruer, prying in every part.*[16]

Besides those[17] strange gestures of staring, frowning, grinning, rolling of eyes, menacing, gastly lookes, broken pace, interrupt, precipitate, halfe turnes. Hee will sometimes sigh, weepe, sob for anger,

NEMPE SUOS IMBRES ETIAM ISTA TONITRUA FUNDUNT,

sweare and belye, slander any man, curse, threaten, brawle, scold,[18] FIGHT; and sometimes againe flatter, and speake faire, aske forgiuenesse, KISSE, AND COLL, CONDEMNE HIS RASHNESSE AND FOLLY, VOW, PROTEST AND SWEARE, HE WILL NEUER DOE SO AGAINE; and then eftsoones,[19] impatient as he is, raue, ROARE, & lay about him like a mad man, THUMPE HER SIDES, DRAGGE HER ABOUT PERCHANCE, DRIUE HER OUT OF DORES, SEND HER HOME, HE WILL BE DIVORCED FORTHWITH, SHE IS A WHORE, &C. BY AND BY WITH ALL SUBMISSE COMPLEMENT, INTREAT HER FAIRE, AND BRING HER IN AGAINE, HE LOUES HER DEARELY, SHEE IS HIS SWEET, MOST KINDE AND LOUING WIFE, HEE WILL NOT CHANGE, NOT LEAUE HER FOR A KINGDOME; SO HE CONTINUES OFF AND ON, AS THE TOY TAKES HIM, THE OBIECT

[12] The preceding bracketed material was added in the fourth edition.
[13] First edition: "ordinary."
[14] Fifth and sixth editions: "or."
[15] Fifth and sixth editions: "into."
[16] Daniel's *Rosamond*, lines 494-95.
[17] First and second editions: "Besides all those."
[18] First edition: "raue."
[19] First and second editions: "againe."

MOUES HIM, BUT MOST PART BRAWLING, FRETTING, VNQUIET HE IS, accusing and suspecting not strangers onely, but Brothers and Sisters, Father, and Mother, nearest & dearest friends. He . . . conceaues vnto himselfe things almost incredible & impossible to be effected. As an Hearne when she[20] fishes, still prying on[21] all sides; *or as a cat doth a mouse, his eye is neuer off hers, hee glotes on him, on her, accurately obseruing on whom she lookes, who lookes at her, what she saith, doth, at dinner, at supper, sitting, walking, at home, abroad, he is the same, still enquiring, mandring,* gazing, listning, affrighted with every *small* obiect [; why did she smile, why did she pity him, commend him? why did she drinke twice to such a man? why did she offer to kisse, to dance? &c. a whore, a whore, an arrant whore.][22] All which he[23] confesseth in the Poet,

Omnia me terrent, timidus sum, ignosce timori . . .

Is't not a man in womans apparell, is not some body in that great chest, or behind the doore, or hangings, or in some of those barrells? May not a man steale[24] in at the window . . .?

This passage is untypical in that it expands almost altogether through the author's independent elaboration. Only one new authority and two embellishing verse quotations are introduced. It admirably illustrates, however, the freedom with which Burton interpolates and his persistence in avoiding alteration of the existing text. The variants recorded in the notes are representative of Burton's minor alterations.

Within the six passages just reviewed, there is no reordering whatsoever. New material is fitted into the existing arrangement, and the text is left unchanged or altered just enough to accommodate the interpolation.

Burton explains, in his fourth and subsequent editions, that he has added much "because many good authors in all kinds are come to my hands" (Shilleto, 1.33).[25] Just as he continues to write his book even after publication, so he continues the studies on which it was based. By examining the expansions in the *Anatomy*, one can learn something about Burton's reading after 1620. Inserted references to works by such authors as Plato, Virgil, Ovid, Plutarch, Lucian, Cardan, Lipsius, etc., obviously do not

[20] First and second editions: "he."
[21] First edition: "of."
[22] Added in the fifth edition.
[23] First and second editions: "As he"; fifth and sixth editions: "All this he."
[24] First and second editions: "come."
[25] A marginal note reads "Frambesarius, Sennertus, Ferandus, &c." Concerning Frambesarius, see below. Burton would probably have made generous use of Jacques Ferrand's *Erotomania* (1612) if he had known it earlier. He goes to some pains to make it clear that he did not see this book until after the publication of his third edition (see 3.67, 223). He owned a copy (edition of Paris, 1623). He read Sennertus also between his third and fourth editions. In the fourth edition he adds his name to those of Lodovicus Mercatus and Rodericus a Castro as an authority on women's diseases (Shilleto, 1.476).

mean that Burton has just read them for the first time. One finds copious quotations from these writers in the first edition. But Burton evidently has read only recently many of the works which he quotes or cites in his additions.

The six parts of the *Anatomy* which I have examined yield several examples of recent reading. In the expansions in the second edition, one finds Hercules de Saxonia's *Tractatus Posthumus de Melancholia*, published in 1620, rather late obviously for mention in the first edition[26]; Sigismundus Scherertzius' *Libellus Consolatorius de Spectris* (1621); Frambesarius' *Canones et Consultationes Medicinales* (1619); Alsarius Crucius' *De Quaesitis per Epistolam in Arte Medica Centuriae Quattuor* (1622); Aristenaetus' *Epistolae Amatoriae*, a Greek romance of the fifth century, to which Burton refers very frequently in the second and subsequent editions; George Buchanan's *Sylvae;* Daniel's *Complaint of Rosamond.*[27] These are mentioned nowhere in the first edition.[28] It is a fair assumption that they constitute a sample of Burton's reading between 1621 and 1624. In the new material in the third edition, books appear which, by the same reasoning, Burton must have read between 1624 and 1628: the treatises on women's diseases by Lodovicus Mercatus and Rodericus a Castro which inspired the subsection on women's melancholies; *Consultationes Medicae* (1618) by Rodericus a Fonseca, professor of medicine at Padua; Johann Nider's *Formicarium*, a pious work of the early fifteenth century (published 1517) from which Burton takes a few bits of information concerning the supernatural; Theodorus Prodromus' metrical romance *Rhodanthe and Dosicles.*[29] In the fourth edition *De Divinatione et Magicis Praestigiis* (?1615) by Jean Jacques Boissard is cited for the first time. There is no certain evidence, in the selected passages, of reading done after 1634. Various new titles appear, however, in other parts of the fifth and sixth editions.[30]

No generalization is possible concerning Burton's reading after 1620

---

[26] Burton uses another work by Hercules, however, in the first edition: *Pantheon de Medicina*, 1603.

[27] Other new authors appearing in the passages in question: Lord Howard, Ambrosius Pareus (Paré), Gaspar Bartholinus, Pineus of Paris. These are mentioned only once in the entire second edition, and Burton adds no references to them in later editions.

[28] No assertion concerning the earliest appearance of a source in the *Anatomy* can represent more than a ninety-nine percent certitude.

[29] The Greek original was published with Latin translation by Gilbert Gualmin in 1625. See Edward Bensly, *Notes and Queries*, ser. X, vol. XI (1909), pp. 101-02.

[30] Hans Jordan Gottlieb, in his unpublished dissertation, "Robert Burton's Knowledge of English Poetry" (New York University, 1936), notes the presence in Burton's last edition of "two couplets from Anthony Hodges' translation of *The Loves of Clitophon and Leucippe* by Achilles Tatius . . . published in Oxford in 1638" (p. 14). John Wilkins' *Discovery of a World in the Moon* is another book published in 1638 which appears in Burton's final edition.

except that, like his earlier reading, it shows that his interests were diversified.[31]

Thus far I have dealt only with additions to the *Anatomy*, more or less substantial. There are also abbreviations and alterations.

Burton does not strive for brevity. In all versions of my selected sections, I have found only one abbreviation which seems to me really meaningful. This is a reduction, in the preface of the third edition, of fifty-two words to nineteen. Burton here softens a complaint concerning his lack of preferment, feeling perhaps that he might appear ungrateful to his patrons. Otherwise I find only four instances of rewriting to abbreviate (seven words reduced to three, four words to two, six words to two, four words to two). I find five outright deletions of more than two words (one of eight words, two of four words, two of three words). This is in material covering fifty odd pages in the Shilleto edition. The abbreviations and deletions are insignificant.[32]

One finds phraseological changes on most pages of the second, third, and fourth editions of the *Anatomy*. To illustrate the character of these, I shall list the revisions (ignoring substantial additions) which occur in successive versions of the subsection concerning witches and magicians. A sentence in the first edition reads: There are "many severall Species of Sorcerers, and Witches, Inchanters, Charmers &c. and haue beene tolerated . . ." In the second edition this becomes: There are "many seuerall Species of Sorcerers, Witches, Inchanters, Charmers, &c. They haue beene tolerated . . ." Farther on, two more *and's* are dropped. (Burton very frequently cuts out *and* and *or*.) To a list of commodities subject to injury by witchcraft, Burton adds "plants," and he supplements "spels, charmes, and barbarous words" with "characters." In revising this second version for his third edition, Burton changes "*Salamanca,* and some other places" to "*Salamanca, Cracouia,* & other places," "was mad" to "was instantly mad," and "such spells" to "those spels." There is no stylistic revision of the passage in the fourth edition. In the fifth edition, Burton changes the statement that witches can cure or cause diseases in "such as they hate" to include "such as they love or hate." No changes appear in the sixth edition. Although he has had five opportunities, Burton has revised this subsection very little.

The successive versions of the other units under consideration contain revisions of a similar character and in something like the same proportional

[31] Hallwachs (see note 10 above) seems to find no clear trend in the new reading which appears in the second edition. He notices, however, that Burton uses the new medical reading to enlarge the non-medical rather than the medical parts of his book (p. 124). In Appendix B he lists the authors whose names appear first in the second edition (132 of them).

[32] Hallwachs finds little excision or abbreviation in the second edition.

number. There are some obviously thoughtful changes.[33] In the second edition, for example, the jealous husband fears that a man may "come in at the window"; in the third edition he fears that a man may "steale in" (see above). In the first edition, love is a "Tragedy"; in later editions, it is a "Tragicomedy" (Shilleto, 3.217). There is occasional sharpening of an idea by addition of words: In the second edition one reads: "Pure water by all meanes vse, which . . ."; in the third edition this becomes: "Pure, thinne, light water by all meanes vse, of good smell and tast, which . . ." (see Shilleto, 2.26). There are many minor alterations of no perceptible importance.

Burton has been credited with serious efforts to improve the style of the *Anatomy* by revision.[34] His revision, it seems to me, is very spotty. There are many insignificant changes, and there are occasional alterations which show sensitiveness to qualities of style and skill in the use of language. For the most part, however, the text is little disturbed except by the insertion of new material. Weaknesses appearing in the first edition, some of which could be easily corrected, remain in the sixth, though Burton has had nineteen years in which to remedy them. He shows that he can improve the text greatly when he tries, but he does not often try. There is no painstaking or thorough reworking of the text of the *Anatomy*.

Burton writes that he has "not revised the copy, and amended the style, which now flows remissly, as it was first conceived, but my leisure would not permit. . . . I should have revised, corrected, and amended this tract; but I had" neither time nor assistance (1.29).[35] I find no sufficient reason to doubt the sincerity or accuracy of this confession (although the excuses seem a little lame). The *Anatomy* gains in stylistic excellence, but the improvement is due almost wholly to the animation, specificness, or eloquence of the insertions.

A general conclusion emerges from the foregoing study-by-sample of the changes in the successive editions of the *Anatomy:* Burton's modifica-

[33] In at least one instance the revision is not motivated by stylistic considerations. In the third and fourth editions, Burton alters the passage in the preface on his years of study at Oxford to fit changing circumstances (1.13).

[34] Hallwachs insists, in his study of the additions and alterations in Burton's second edition, upon "the deliberate care" and "conscious artistry" (p. 172) of Burton's revision. He finds the additions much more numerous than the alterations, yet he considers the stylistic changes significant. He presents a great many examples to show that Burton took pains in the improvement of diction and syntax, in the employment of rhetorical devices, and in the production of rhythmic effects. He points out a few passages in which Burton has effectively rearranged material. (There are no rearrangements at all in the sections which I have examined closely.) When one remembers, however, that Hallwachs is discussing revisions spread through 652 folio pages, the evidence seems less impressive.

[35] Part of this appears in the postscript of the first edition; all of it in the preface of the second and later editions.

tion of his text is almost altogether amplification. He discards extremely little. In the sections under study, he never rearranges. He makes comparatively few phraseological changes. Even in making an insertion, he disturbs the existing text little or none at all. In the 1624 preface he writes: "Some things are heere altered, expunged in this Edition, others amended; much added," and he allows this statement to stand in subsequent editions (Shilleto, 1.33). It is easier to find the additions than the deletions and alterations which he says he has made.

The augmentation, furthermore, is one of size rather than of substance. Burton's additions consist principally of elaborations upon ideas already present in the first edition. Just as he adds no new sections or subsections to his book (with the single exception noted), so he adds few ideas within the subsections. His book is much richer for his additions, but he has said substantially what he has to say in his first edition.

It is not surprising that he failed to develop new interests and opinions after 1620, for in that year he reached the age of forty-three. Both his view of life and his book, however, might have reached their relatively final form considerably earlier. The expansion through elaboration that one can trace through the successive editions of the *Anatomy* could have been going on for some years before 1620. At some indeterminable earlier date, the author worked out his plan, wrote his outlines, and arranged the material already at hand. From that time forward, the book changed little except by accretion. It became longer, livelier, and richer but not fundamentally different.

IV

A great deal of work went into the composition of the *Anatomy*. The author busied himself "in this playing labour" (1.18) to avoid the idleness which aggravates melancholy. His leisure seems to have been abundant, but the gathering and fitting together of the material in the first edition would have kept him occupied through several years. By the time the treatise was ready for the printer, the habit of working on it had apparently become so firmly established that he could not stop. His repeated assertion, in the third and later editions, that he will do no more with his book suggests a growing weariness with his life-long, self-imposed task. Yet he continued to work at the book, with slowly diminishing industry, for the rest of his life.

His assiduity in compilation indicates that he enjoyed gathering and arranging and proves that he was not a lazy man. The labors of stylistic trimming and polishing, however, seem to have been distasteful to him. He was strongly disinclined also to anything like a general reorganization. "Carpenters do find out of experience," he writes, " 'tis much better build a new sometimes than repair an old house." But he did not build anew. "I could as soon write as much more, as alter that which is written" (1.32). He is like a man who builds a house and who for many years thereafter continues to work at it, strengthening it a little here, adding something ornamental there, not altogether satisfied with the workmanship or the fundamental plan but reluctant to begin over. His unwillingness to revise his plan and reorder his material explains some of the incongruities of the *Anatomy*.

As his treatise of melancholy spread into tangential subjects, Burton perhaps should have made some changes. Perhaps he should have decided upon two separate projects. Perhaps he should have redesigned his work so as to subordinate the psychiatric material to the critical comment. If he had done so, the real significance of the *Anatomy* would be much clearer. But he had little taste for doing anything over. He justified the inclusion of a general characterization of human behavior in a psychiatric treatise on the ground that the world's unreasonableness is the world's melancholy and left the framework unaltered. Once the book had reached a fairly definite form at some date earlier than 1620, it grew like a vegetable.

The *Anatomy* is not just the book which Burton originally planned to write. In the book which he actually produced, a purpose is superimposed upon a purpose. He has written something which is both a psychiatric treatise and a commentary upon men and manners. Many readers doubtless have been confused by the resulting duality, and some may have felt that disunity was a serious weakness in the book.[36]

The *Anatomy* is organized as a treatise on melancholy, but its real achievement lies in the superimposed criticism of human behavior. It may be that Burton should have done it differently. But if he had planned and written more rationally and deliberately, his book might have lacked a good deal of the spontaneity and the peculiar flavor that it has. It is doubtful, in any case, that the author, being Robert Burton, could have written otherwise than as he did.

v

The fact that the *Anatomy* exists in six versions, or stages of amplification, makes the preparation of a definitive scholar's edition unusually difficult. The simultaneous presentation of all the texts is a problem of format which is possibly beyond solution. There would be also the task of annotation. To trace all of Burton's quotations and citations to their sources, to correct all of his errors, and to explain all of his obscure references would require years of dedicated labor (and generous funds for travel).

[36] Siegbert Prawer, in "Burton's 'Anatomy of Melancholy,'" *Cambridge Journal*, I (1947-48), 671-88, makes the point that Burton the raconteur is at cross-purposes with Burton the medical writer. He fails to see the more fundamental reason for the duality of the *Anatomy*.

In 1910 Edward Bensly published the information that "W. Aldis Wright has made a collation of all the editions [of the *Anatomy*] from 1621 to 1676; his work is not yet published."[37] Wright died in 1914. In 1927 Bensly announced that "the collations and other materials of the late Dr. W. Aldis Wright . . . have been kindly lent me by the Council of Trinity College, Cambridge, for the preparation of an edition of *The Anatomy of Melancholy* to be published by the Clarendon Press under the joint names of Dr. Wright and myself."[38] Bensly died in 1938. There has been no further announcement concerning a definitive edition.

We shall probably use the existing editions for some time to come. All of these are reprints of the completed *Anatomy*. All of them have their shortcomings.

The three-volume edition of the Reverend A. R. Shilleto (1893)[39] is the best known and may be considered the standard edition. Its deficiencies have been well advertised by Bensly. Unfortunately Shilleto based his text on the seventh edition, assuming that it was an accurate reprint of the sixth. His vagaries of spelling, capitalization, and punctuation result in a text which is neither Burtonian nor modern. He often corrects Burton's misquotations silently. As Bensly has pointed out, there are many factual errors in his notes. Yet he supplies a text which for most purposes will do, and he has identified a great many of Burton's unidentified quotations.

In preparing their all-English edition of the *Anatomy* (two volumes, New York, 1927; reprinted as one volume, 1928), Paul Jordan-Smith and Floyd Dell have performed a welcome service for a generation lacking in classical languages. The index, which identifies many of the obscure sources, is a very helpful tool for the study of Burton. The translation of the Latin and the omission of the marginalia, however, make this edition unsuitable for some scholarly purposes.

The edition of Holbrook Jackson (three volumes, Everyman's Library, 1932) is an accurate reproduction of Burton's sixth edition (spelling and punctuation modernized) with bracketed translations of most of the Latin. It is awkward to have Burton's notes separated from the text, and it is unfortunate that the editor has supplied very few notes of his own to explain or identify. Yet Jackson's edition is the modern reprint which most closely approximates the *Anatomy* as Burton left it.

[37] *Cambridge History of English Literature*, IV, 566.
[38] "Some Alterations and Errors in Successive Editions of *The Anatomy of Melancholy*," *Oxford Bibliographical Society Proceedings and Papers*, I (1922-26), 215.
[39] Reprinted in the Bohn Library 1896, 1903, 1926-27. The introduction is by A. H. Bullen.

Chapter III: THE AUTHOR

ROBERT BURTON was an Oxford fellow and a clergyman.[1] He was born at Lindley, Leicestershire, February 8, 1577, "of worshipful parents . . . an ancient family" (2.165), the fourth of nine children. He matriculated at Brasenose College, Oxford, in 1593, transferred to Christ Church College in 1599, and received his B. A. from Christ Church in 1602 at the relatively late age of twenty-six. Evidently his studies were seriously interrupted between 1593 and 1599, perhaps by the prolonged illness which, it is supposed, initiated his melancholy. He received his M. A. degree from Christ Church in 1605, his B. D. in 1614, and spent the rest of his life there as tutor and librarian. In the *Anatomy* he refers to Oxford residents and patrons, to occurrences at Oxford, and to features of Oxford life. Beyond showing that he felt a loyal affection for his university and that he was much alive to what was happening around him, these references do not add significantly to our knowledge of his life and character.

In 1616 he was appointed vicar of St. Thomas, in the suburbs of Oxford. From 1624 to 1631 he was also rector of Walesby in Lincolnshire,[2] a living in the gift of Frances, Countess Dowager of Exeter. He resigned this benefice, he says "for some special reasons" (2.79). The evasive vagueness of the phrase suggests some bitterness. At some time between 1632 and 1635, he was appointed to the living of Seagrave in Leicestershire by George Lord Berkeley (2.73), to whom all editions of the *Anatomy* are dedicated. Anthony Wood says that Burton kept the Oxford and Leicestershire livings "with much ado to his dying day."[3] He conducted services in St. Thomas but apparently held the other livings as absentee.[4]

Aside from two brief Latin poems, his earliest known literary effort was a contribution to *Alba*, a pastoral comedy presented before King James during his visit to Oxford in late August, 1605.[5] The royal spectators

[1] The known facts concerning Burton's life are rather few. For more details, see especially Fox, *Book of Bachelors*, pp. 398-408; Jordan-Smith, *Bibliographia Burtoniana*, pp. 7-15; Bergen Evans, *The Psychiatry of Robert Burton* (New York, 1944), pp. 5-15.
[2] See Jordan-Smith, *Bibliographia Burtoniana*, pp. 8-9.
[3] *Athenae Oxonienses*, ed. Bliss, II, 652.
[4] Burton's concern over his rights in a certain field which he used to pasture his horse indicates that he visited Seagrave rather often. Yet he had a curate at Seagrave. See Paul Jordan-Smith, "Footnote Smith," *American Book Collector*, April 1957, p. 3.
[5] Henry N. Paul, in *The Royal Play of Macbeth* (New York, 1950), p. 17, quotes from a letter which Burton wrote to his brother William on August 11, 1605. In this Burton refers to his share in the play: The part which he has written "is well liked, especially those scenes of the Magus." I have not been able to trace this letter. Paul erroneously states that *Alba* was published in 1862. The play is not extant.

were not amused. According to a visitor from Cambridge who apparently saw the performance, "The Comedy began between nine and ten, and ended at one. . . . In the acting thereof they brought in five or six men almost naked, which were much disliked by the Queen and Ladies, and also many rusticall songes and dances, which made it very tedious, insomuch that if the Chancellors of both Universities had not intreated his Majesty earnestly, he would have gone before half the Comedy had been ended."[6] But Burton seems to have been undiscouraged by the royal displeasure, for in 1606 he wrote his Latin comedy *Philosophaster*,[7] which he revised for performance at Christ Church College on February 6, 1617/18 (1.375). Burton's extant works are the *Anatomy, Philosophaster*, and nineteen Latin poems.

Burton died January 25, 1640, very near the time which he had predicted astrologically. According to Wood, the Oxford students whispered among themselves that he had committed suicide in order to validate his prediction. He had written his own epitaph: "Paucis notus paucioribus ignotus hic iacet Democritus Iunior cui vitam dedit et mortem melancholia."

Wood characterizes Burton as an accomplished and industrious scholar, "a devourer of authors, a melancholy and humorous person . . . of great honesty, plain dealing and charity. I have heard some of the antients of Ch. Ch. often say that his company was very merry, facete and juvenile" and that his conversation was prized "for his ready and dextrous interlarding" of it "with verses from the poets or sentences from classical authors."[8]

Since he is quoting the elders of Christ Church, Wood's characterization is probably accurate, but it is scanty. The bits of information concerning Burton's personality which later authors furnish are not dependable.[9] The *Anatomy*, however, tells us a great deal about its author. In

---

[6] John Nichols, *The Progresses . . . of King James* (London, 1828), I, 547-48.

[7] Two manuscripts of *Philosophaster* exist. A note on one of these gives the date of original composition. The play was first published in 1862 for the Roxburghe Club (ed. W. E. Buckley). Paul Jordan-Smith has made it generally available with an English translation: *Robert Burton's Philosophaster . . . with His Other Minor Writings* (Stanford, Cal., 1931). This volume includes the Latin poems, all but one of which appear also in the Roxburghe volume.

Philosophaster was performed on the campus of the University of California, Los Angeles, in January, 1930. Jordan-Smith's translation was used.

[8] Pp. 652-53.

[9] In Bishop White Kennett's *Register and Chronicle* (1728), one reads, for example, that nothing could make Burton laugh "but going down to the Bridge-foot in *Oxford*, and hearing the Barge-men scold and storm and swear at one another, at which he would set his Hands to his Sides, and laugh most profusely" (edition of 1744, pp. 320-321). Commentators have found this passage interesting because it suggests that Burton was imitating the laughter of his prototype Democritus at what he saw in the harbor of ancient Abdera (see *Anatomy*, 1.13). There were no barges on the Thames as high as Oxford, however, until August 1635 (see Charles E. Mallet, *A History of the University of Oxford*, London, 1924, II, 312). Would Burton have begun such an eccentric practice at the age of fifty-eight?

31

dealing with his self-revelations, I shall distinguish between the character which he assumes ("Democritus Junior") and the character of the man himself.

To Burton's literate contemporaries, the name Democritus would have suggested "laughing philosopher." They knew that Democritus was a pre-Socratic thinker, a cosmologist, and the proponent of an atomic theory of matter. But references to him in Renaissance works usually represent him as the eccentric laugher, the scoffer, the perceptive and satiric critic of man and society. Erasmus' *Folly*, for example, declares that "It would take a thousand Democrituses to laugh at [human absurdities] properly— and then there would be work for one more Democritus to laugh at the laughers."[10] Over a century later, James Shirley takes advantage of the same associations in recommending the comedies in the first Beaumont and Fletcher folio: "Would thy Melancholy have a cure? thou shalt laugh at *Democritus* himselfe . . ."[11] Certain titles of the period use the name Democritus to suggest mirthful or satiric content, for example Samuel Rowlands' *Democritus, or Doctor Merry Man, His Medicine Against Melancholy Humours* (London, 1607).[12] Indeed Burton suspects that his pseudonym may suggest "a pasquil, a satire" (1.11).

Renaissance writers often mention Democritus in company with Heraclitus, "the weeping philosopher," in whom human vice and folly continually excited tears.[13] Both are considered melancholy men; both are regarded as men of keen perception and profound wisdom. They react antithetically, each according to his character and the variety of his melancholy, to the same sorry spectacle.

Democritus' reputation as the laughing philosopher was due largely to the wide circulation of the "Hippocratic letters," supposed to come from the correspondence of Hippocrates of Cos, the great physician of anti-

[10] *The Praise of Folly*, tr. and ed. Leonard F. Dean (New York, 1946), p. 88. Burton refers to this passage (1.53-54). Cf. *Praise of Folly*, pp. 37, 64.

[11] From Shirley's foreword "To the Reader," *The Works of Francis Beaumont and John Fletcher*, ed. Glover-Waller (Cambridge, 1905-12), I, xii.

[12] There is an anonymous *Riddles of Heraclitus and Democritus* (London, 1598). The title is doubtfully appropriate to the content. (Concerning Democritus' association with Heraclitus, see below.) *Democritus His Dreame* (London, 1605), a satiric poem by Peter Woodhouse, introduces Democritus and Heraclitus as contrasting characters (reprinted in *Occasional Issues of Unique or Very Rare Books*, vol. III [1877], ed. A. B. Grosart). Burton owned copies of two editions (1616, 1618) of *Democritus Christianus* by Petrus Bessaeus. He refers to this work once in the *Anatomy* (1.12). I have found seven later seventeenth century titles which use the name of Democritus.

[13] Some examples from readily accessible sources: Montaigne, *Essais*, I, 50; Timothy Bright, *Treatise of Melancholie*, p. 149; Sir Thomas Browne, *Religio Medici, Works*, ed. Geoffrey Keynes (London, 1928-30), I, 79; Thomas Fuller's entry on Shakespeare in the *Worthies*. The Democritus-Heraclitus antithesis was evidently a familiar idea as early as the time of Lucian. See the Loeb *Lucian*, II, 473-77; III, 170-71; V, 9. Concerning the melancholy of Heraclitus, see Diogenes Laertius' *Lives*, IX, vi.

quity.[14] Modern scholarship regards these as spurious, but apparently their authenticity was seldom questioned during the Renaissance. Eight of the letters, some written by Hippocrates, others addressed to him, concern a journey which Hippocrates made to Abdera to attempt the cure of Democritus' supposed madness; four more are letters later exchanged by these two famous men; others concern other matters.

In his satirical preface (1.48-53) Burton tells the story of Hippocrates' journey to Abdera and reviews the content of the longest of the letters, an epistle from Hippocrates to his friend Damagetus giving a detailed account of his reception in Abdera and of his interview with Democritus. Burton says that he has reproduced the "Epistle to *Damagetus . . . verbatim* almost" (1.48). This statement is misleading, for he has greatly condensed the original, and the translation is very free. Yet his version represents the original closely enough.

As Burton tells the story, Democritus' continual laughter, on even the most solemn occasions, had led his fellow citizens of Abdera to believe him mad, and in their deep solicitude for him they had summoned the famous physician. Hippocrates found the patient alone in his garden, a book on his knees, dissecting animals to discover, if he could, *"the cause of madness and melancholy,"* that is, of the universally irrational behavior of mankind. When the doctor questioned him about his apparently unwarranted mirth, Democritus replied that he laughed "at the vanity and fopperies of the time, to see men so empty of all virtuous actions," devoting their lives to frivolous purposes (1.49). There follows a long satiric discourse, interrupted once by remonstrances from Hippocrates, in which Democritus elaborates scornfully on the idea of human folly with copious exemplification. At a late hour of the day Hippocrates reluctantly took his leave and told the anxious Abderites that "the world had not a wiser, a more learned, a more honest man" than Democritus, "and they were much deceived to say that he was mad" (1.53).

Democritus dominates the prefatory pages of the *Anatomy*. He first appears on the fontispiece-title-page. His picture here shows him seated beneath a tree in a despondent or contemplative attitude with a peculiarly flaccid book across his knees. Around him lie the bodies of animals; "The Argument of the Frontispiece" explains that of these "he makes Anatomy, The seat of Black Choler to see" (1.2). The sign of "*Saturn* Lord of Melancholy" is inscribed above him. His name recurs throughout the

---

[14] The Greek text of these is reproduced with French translation in *Oeuvres Complètes d'Hippocrate*, ed. É. Littré (Paris, 1839-61), IX, 312-429. Littré lists eight Latin translations of the letters, some printed more than once, which Burton could have used (IX, 310-12). Burton did not use a Greek text.

For discussion of the authenticity of the letters, see Littré, IX, 308-09. Burton refers once to this question (3.308), but he apparently does not seriously doubt that the epistles are genuine.

satirical preface. At the close of the preface comes a Latin address to the reader which concerns the satiric powers which Democritus Junior has inherited from his spiritual ancestor. Latin verses appended to this contrast Democritus and Heraclitus. The references to Democritus scattered through the *Anatomy* proper are very numerous. Some of these pair him with Heraclitus.

Burton is acquainted with Democritus' atomic theory and with his cosmological ideas (1.11, 2.57-63). He seems greatly interested in his hypothesis of infinite worlds. To Burton, however, Democritus is primarily the satiric commentator represented in the Hippocratic letters, the "common flouter of folly" (1.127), rather than the philosopher or natural scientist.

From time to time he drops bits of information concerning Democritus which he has gathered from a variety of sources, most often from Diogenes Laertius' *Lives* (IX, 7) and from the Hippocratic epistles. Democritus "was a little wearish old man" (1.12), wrinkled, melancholic, much addicted in his later years to contemplative solitude and to study (1.12, 284, 455; 3.27). He wrote a book entitled *Diacosmos*. He was regarded as an authority on husbandry by Columella and Constantinus (1.12). In his youth "he travelled to *Egypt* and *Athens*, to confer with learned men." Later he settled in Abdera in Thrace, having been sent for "to be their Law-maker, Recorder or Town-clerk as some will; or as others, he was there bred and born" (1.13). In later life he was blind (2.155). He put out his own eyes because he wished to devote himself wholly to contemplation (1.13), "because he could not abide to see wicked men prosper" (3.454), because he lusted after women and "was much troubled to see that which he might not enjoy" (3.357).[15] He "lived by the smell of bread alone, applied to his nostrils, for some few days, when for old age he could eat no meat" (2.288).

Democritus left his projected book on melancholy "unperfect, and it is now lost"; this project Democritus Junior undertakes "to revive again, prosecute and finish, in this treatise" (1.17). The *Anatomy* is the work which Democritus planned, which he was preparing when Hippocrates saw him, but which he did not complete. Robert Burton makes it clear that he has much in common with the Democritus of the Hippocratic letters and should therefore be well qualified to be his successor.

The pseudo-Hippocrates writes that Democritus, a man without family ties, seeks out lonely places and lives with his own intense cogitations. He is clearly afflicted with melancholy.[16] Burton is also a melancholy man (the melancholy planet "*Saturn* was the Lord of my geniture," 1.14) and

[15] Various ancient authors refer to Democritus' self-blinding. See especially Aulus Gellius, *Attic Nights*, X, xvii. The idea that lust was the reason was Tertullian's (*Apology*, XLVI).

[16] *Oeuvres*, IX, 330-31. Cf. *Anatomy*, 1.455.

a solitary man: "I live still a Collegiate student, as *Democritus* in his garden, and lead a monastick life . . . *no wife nor children*" (1.14-15). He permits his reader to suppose that he has both the profundity and the eccentricity of his prototype.

Democritus' melancholy, says Burton, was of the sanguine variety (1.461). The sanguine melancholy is a mental abnormality due to a melancholy humor arising from the corruption of blood. It manifests itself in spells of high exhilaration and gaiety alternating cyclically with fits of deepest depression.[17] I believe that Burton considered himself also a sanguine melancholic. He has a good deal to say in the *Anatomy* about the ups and downs of melancholy (*e.g.*, in "The Author's Abstract of Melancholy," 1.9-10) with the implication that he himself has experienced them.

Democritus' isolation from men and their affairs gave him critical perspective. Burton enjoys a like advantage, for he lives "sequestered from those tumults & troubles of the world," which he watches as if from "some high place above you all . . . A mere spectator of other men's fortunes and adventures" and of all the turbulence and calamity of human life (1.15). Like Democritus he is a perceptive, reflective, and amused onlooker who sees human events and their significance more clearly than any participant could. Lucian's Menippus, another detached and animatedly critical spectator, might be a secondary prototype for Burton. His name appears several times in the *Anatomy*.

The Hippocratic letters indicate that Democritus reacted to the spectacle of man's unreason not only with laughter but with fluent satire. Most of the letter to Damagetus consists of the characterization of human behavior which Democritus delivers. The style of this is vigorously derisive and chaotically profuse: Although men

wish to be masters of great domains, they cannot rule themselves. They hasten to marry women whom soon after they reject. They love, they hate. They desire children; then, when these are grown, drive them forth. . . . I laugh . . . at their misfortunes, for they violate the principles of truth. Rivaling one another in hatred, they quarrel with brothers, parents, fellow citizens over possessions of which no man after death can continue to be master. They gorge themselves. They show their wickedness in their indifference to the needs of their friends and their country. They devote riches to unworthy and inanimate things. At the price of all they possess, they buy skillfully wrought statues because these seem capable of speech; yet they hate those who speak truly. . . . they are conquered daily by debauchery, by

[17] See *Anatomy*, 1.460, and *Elizabethan Malady*, pp. 33-36. A melancholy disorder due to any corrupted natural humor would be likely to have a cyclic character, the symptoms at the "high" point of the cycle varying according to the variety of the humor.

love of money, by all the passions with which their souls are sick. All exemplify the nature of Thersites. Why, Hippocrates, do you rebuke my laughter?[18]

This is only a fraction of Democritus' tirade.

Burton is also the mocking laugher and critic. He warns his reader that Democritus Junior will be his "censor and accuser, [and] being of petulant spleen, will inundate you with jokes, crush you with witticisms, and sacrifice you . . . to the God of Laughter." If the reader is disposed to cavil, some friend may remind him of Hippocrates' pronouncement concerning Democritus' supposed madness: "You, Democritus, are wise, it is the people of Abdera that are foolish and mad."[19] In the *Anatomy* there are many pages of scoffing invective which give the same impression of energetic spontaneity that one finds in Democritus' discourse. Burton's indignant catalogs of human follies and iniquities are much like those of the Hippocratic epistle.

The reason for Democritus' study of melancholy was his perception of the fact that human misery arises from human unreason and folly, that is, from man's madness, his melancholy. He was seeking a cure for the madness of mankind, a preventive for man's self-inflicted misery (see *Anatomy* 1.17). "I do anatomize and cut up these poor beasts, to see these distempers, vanities, and follies, yet such proof were better made on man's body, if my kind nature would endure it: who from the hour of his birth is most miserable, weak, and sickly; when he sucks he is guided by others, when he is grown great practiseth unhappiness, and is sturdy, and when old, a child again, and repenteth him of his life past" (*Anatomy*, I, 52). Beneath Democritus' scornful levity there is compassion, and this is the primary motivation of his researches. Burton likewise, perceiving that man's unhappiness is due to his failure in reasonable self-control (see Chap. VII), has pursued his study of melancholy to aid his fellows as well as himself, to perform a service for this lunatic world (1.19, 37, 159, 200). He jeers at the absurdities and sins of men, but he also understands and sympathizes. "I hate their vices, not their persons" (1.139). "I did sometimes laugh and scoff with *Lucian*, and satirically tax with *Menippus*, [but sometimes] lament with *Heraclitus*" (1.16).

Burton's pen name admirably expresses the character of his book. The *Anatomy* is just such a work as the Hippocratic Democritus might have written. It is a treatise on melancholy written by a melancholy man, containing technical information on causes, symptoms, and cures. It finds the primary cause of man's unhappiness in man's unreason. It lengthily depicts the follies of human life with satiric pungency and extravagance. The pseudonym expresses also the role in which Burton wishes to present him-

[18] *Oeuvres*, IX, 360-65. The translation is mine. Cf. *Anatomy*, 1.49-50.
[19] Burton's Latin address to the reader, 1.143-44 (Shilleto's translation).

self: the intelligent, detached, and reflective onlooker who must laugh with Democritus lest he weep with Heraclitus. The role is assumed but is by no means foreign to Burton's actual personality.

II

Burton is not so self-effacing as his use of a pseudonym might suggest. Although the author's name does not appear on the title page of the first or of any subsequent seventeenth century edition of his book, his identity was never really hidden. The first edition closes with a postscript signed "Robert Bvrton," "From my Studie in *Christ-Church* Oxon. Decemb. 5. 1620." In this addendum Burton explains that, although he at first intended anonymity, he has decided for unspecified "reasons" to acknowledge his authorship. The signed postscript appears in no other edition; but in all editions there are identifying details in the text itself such as references to members of the author's family (he names five of them in the second and later editions), to his birthplace and childhood home (2.79, 290), to the grammar school of his youth (2.73), and to friends and patrons. The engraved title page of the third and later editions includes his picture. He writes as Democritus Junior to gain "a little more liberty and freedom of speech" and to stress the fact that he has taken up the task of the elder Democritus (1.16-17). He uses the pseudonym to suggest a role, not to disguise himself.

He makes no real effort to conceal his personality, his preoccupations, or the circumstances of his life; indeed, he seems very candid in self-disclosure. The Robert Burton that emerges from the book is much more than a latter day Democritus.[20]

He is an obscure man who leads an uneventful, bookish life. He is not wealthy; all his "treasure is in *Minerva's* tower" (1.14). He has rich and influential friends and might with their help have pushed ahead in the world, but he has not pressed them for favors (1.14, 362-63). He has "had enough, and more peradventure than I deserved" (1.363). He is not aggressive. If he had "been as forward and ambitious as some others," he would have published his sermons, but he prefers "to suppress [his] labours in this kind" (1.34).

Yet he is resigned rather than contented in his obscurity. He is grateful, he says, to his "bountiful patrons, and noble benefactors," but his place in life does not match his "desire." "And now as a mired horse, that

---

[20] I have not looked for unconscious self-revelations in the *Anatomy*. Bergen Evans, reading between the lines, makes various discoveries, for example that Burton's personality was warped by a childhood belief that he was unloved and rejected (see *The Psychiatry of Robert Burton*, especially pp. 6-7, 16, 24). This possibly is quite true, but the evidence for it is tenuous. Evans suggests also that Burton was prompted by discontentment with his cloistered existence to seek to "identify himself" with "a virile world" (p. 15). The supporting evidence is hardly solid, but I am willing to believe this simply because the impulse is so common among academics.

37

struggles at first with all his might and main to get out, but when he sees no remedy, that his beating will not serve, lies still, I have laboured in vain, rest satisfied" (2.217-18).

Without question he suffers deeply from a sense of frustration.[21] In many passages of the *Anatomy* he rails at the prosperity of the stupid and unworthy. Evidently he feels that he and his kind have been unwisely and unjustly excluded from the affairs of the world and its rewards (see Chap. VII). They are denied the opportunity to perform the services that they could and should perform: "we that are University men . . . are never used: or, as too many candles, illuminate ourselves alone" (1.373). In Burton's utopia the most honorable and responsible posts are occupied by scholars (1.116). But in the sorry world of reality they must be contented with conversation with one another, with self-devised occupations, and with their private thoughts. To avoid slothful idleness, Burton has busied himself in the "playing labour" of writing the *Anatomy;* he feels that he is like those who *"recite to trees, & declaim to pillars"* (1.18).

Although he leads a "monastick life," Burton is very much alive to the charm of women. He writes an essay on feminine beauty, with attention both to the parts and to the whole (3.89-96). This, however, might be based altogether on his reading. He seems to be writing from experience when he recommends innocent pleasures for their therapeutic value: "Beauty alone is a sovereign remedy against fear, grief, and all melancholy fits . . . sweet smells, good diet, touch, taste, embracing, singing, dancing, sports, plays, and, above the rest, exquisite beauties . . . to meet, or see a fair maid pass by, or to be in company with her" (2.138). Although plainness insures fidelity, "I had rather marry a fair one, and put it to the hazard, than be troubled with a blowze" (3.352).

He writes feelingly of marital happiness (3.58), argues lengthily for marriage (3.282-92), and extends hearty good wishes to all bridal couples: "God give them joy together! . . . they both excel in gifts of body and mind . . . youth, vigor, alacrity, she is fair and lovely as *Lais* or *Helena,* he as another *Cleinias* or *Alcibiades"* (3.293). As an Oxford fellow, Burton could not marry. He does not specifically complain of the restriction laid upon himself and his colleagues, yet he clearly believes that scholars should marry (3.285).

He has a keen perception, which I think is unusual for his period, of the miseries and evils which arise from sexual suppressions and prohibitions. He denounces the rule of celibacy imposed upon its clergy by the Roman Catholic Church: it is "against the laws of nature, opposite to religion, policy, and humanity, so to starve, to offer violence [to,] to suppress the vigour of youth . . . to debar them of that to which by their innate tem-

---

[21] This point is emphasized by Murry, "Burton's 'Anatomy,'" pp. 39-44, and by Evans, *Psychiatry of Robert Burton,* pp. 19-24.

perature they are so furiously inclined, urgently carried . . ." (1.480; see also 1.481, 3.280-83). He censures the folly of parents who, ("now cold and decrepit themselves," delay and hinder their children's marriages: "they will stifle nature, their young bloods must not participate of youthful pleasures" (3.270). He seems to approve of controlled prostitution (3.283).

In writing on woman and love, he is not altogether at ease (see 1.480). He devotes nine pages to defending his treatise on love melancholy from possible charges of frivolity and lasciviousness (3.1-9). He confesses, furthermore, that his experience has not been such as to qualify him as a writer on love: "I am but a novice, a Contemplator only . . . yet *homo sum, &c.* not altogether inexpert in this subject . . . what I say is merely reading, *ex aliorum forsan ineptiis,* by mine own observation, and others' relation" (3.212). His consciousness of inexperience, however, does not deter him from writing two hundred and fifty extravagant pages on the subject of love between the sexes or from frequent discourse (sometimes intimately physiological) on femininity.

Burton's interest in women and his apparent desire for a woman's love must, under his personal circumstances, have deepened his feeling of frustration. He seems, however, to have found compensations. Throughout the *Anatomy* he exhibits an enthusiasm for simple amusements, nowhere more clearly, of course, than in his section on recreations as a cure for melancholy (2.80 ff). Here he discourses on tennis, hunting, fowling, fishing, archery; sight-seeing excursions, plays, athletic contests; indoor games, story-telling, gossiping; maskings and mummings, etc. Mirth and merry company—"pleasant discourse, jests, conceits, merry tales" (2.137) —are effective antidotes for melancholy. He approves of gambling in moderation (2.95-96), apparently even of cock-fighting and bear-baiting (3.429n). He warmly defends "honest disports" as "good and lawful things . . . Feasts, mirth, musick, hawking, hunting, singing, dancing, &c." (3.429).

He has great enthusiasm for music ("divine Musick," 2.134), which he continually associates with gaiety. He displays none of the technical knowledge of music, however, that one might expect of a cultivated Jacobean. He was apparently no musician.

In general he gives the impression of being the spectator rather than the participant in recreations. He probably never indulged in some of those which he recommends and praises (was he a tennis player?) and certainly he had scant opportunity for others. It is clear, nevertheless, that he had a huge enthusiasm for pastimes, conviviality, and laugher and that he had a great capacity for enjoyment.

Burton reacts strongly to sensuous beauty of all kinds. He has the poet's sensitivity without any ability in metrical phrasing. He delights in pleasant prospects (2.78-79) and in walking "amongst Orchards, Gardens, Bowers . . . betwixt wood and water, in a fair meadow, by a river side, *ubi variae avium cantationes, florum colores, pratorum frutices, &c."* (2.86). He praises the beauty of the opulent palaces of which he has read (2.87-88); he believes that it refreshes "the soul of man, to see fair-built Cities, Streets, Theatres, Temples, Obelisks, &c." (2.88). He is moved by "beauty in all things . . . a fair hawk, a fine garment . . . Whiteness in the Lily, red in the Rose, purple in the Violet, a lustre in all things without life, the clear light of the Moon, the bright beams of the Sun, splendour of Gold, purple, sparkling Diamond, the excellent feature of the Horse, the Majesty of the Lion, the colour of Birds, Peacocks' tails, the silver scales of Fish" (3.73-74).

Any sort of variegated or animated spectacle attracts and pleases him: "to see passengers go by in some great roadway, or boats in a river, *in subjectum forum despicere*, to oversee a Fair, a Market place, or out of a pleasant window into some thorough-fare street, to behold a continual concourse, a promiscuous rout, coming and going, or a multitude of spectators at a Theatre, a Mask, or some such like shew" (2.79). He finds it most pleasant "to make a petty progress, a merry journey now and then with some good companions, to visit friends, see Cities, Castles, Towns" (2.86).

Some "count him unhappy that never travelled, a kind of prisoner" (2.78). Burton himself has never actually travelled abroad (1.14), but he has read a great deal of cosmographical and travel literature (see especially 2.40 ff., 70-79, 84-90). He enjoys this kind of travel in imagination keenly. What greater pleasure can there be, he asks, "than to view those elaborate Maps of *Ortelius, Mercator, Hondius*, &c. [?] To peruse those books of Cities, put out by *Braunus* and *Hogenbergius*? To read those exquisite descriptions of *Maginus, Munster* . . . ? Those famous expeditions of *Christo. Columbus, Amerigo Vespucci, Marcus Polus*, the *Venetian* . . .? those accurate diaries of *Portugese, Hollanders* . . . *Hakluyt's* Voyages, *Pet. Martyr's Decades, Benzo* . . . *Sands, &c.* to *Jerusalem, Egypt*, and other remote places of the world?" (2.103). A great deal of what he has learned from ancient and modern authors about the natural features, the people, the religions, and the social customs of many lands is incorporated in the *Anatomy*. He seems particularly interested in China, Turkey, Egypt, and the lands of northern Europe.

He is fascinated not only by the exotic and remote but also by the bizarre. He is an industrious collector of incredibilities: the Japanese god that deflowers a maiden each month (3.52), palm trees mutually enamoured (3.47), the ship dug out of a Swiss mountain containing the carcasses of forty-eight men (2.47), showers of "Stones, Frogs, Mice, &c. Rats" (2.55). In the digression of spirits, one reads of many astonishing matters: *e.g.*, of how Jerome Cardan's father "conjured up 7 Devils in

40

Greek apparel" and learned from them "that they lived & died as men did, save that they were far longer liv'd, (700 or 800. years)" (1.210). This same Fazio Cardan had a familiar spirit, "an aerial Devil, bound to him for twenty and eight years. As *Agrippa's* dog had a Devil tied to his collar; some think that *Paracelsus* (or else *Erastus* belies him) had one confined to his sword pummel; others wear them in rings, &c." (1.218-19).

In the more strictly psychiatric parts of the *Anatomy* one finds many tales of strange hallucinations. There is a tale of a man who, because of flatulent rumblings in his viscera, thought that he had frogs in his belly. Before he found relief, he studied physic for seven years at one university after another seeking the cause of his ailment and the remedy for it (1.474). There are stories of men who think that they are kings and emperors, of men who have strange notions concerning their own persons —they are wolves, dogs, bears; they are made of glass, of butter—, of men who see ecstatic visions and believe themselves prophets.

In the "Digression of the Air" Burton makes an imaginary aerial journey through the world to investigate the many wonders of which he has read. If he could actually make such an investigation, the disillusionments would be painful to him, for he gets great imaginative pleasure from the contemplation of the marvelous. He probably would rather believe than doubt that there are "birds that live continually in the air, and are never seen on ground but dead" (2.57n).

Burton has other qualities of mind and personality that inspire more confidence than this imaginative naïveté. Probably the fundamental characteristic of his thinking is moderation. He continually avoids excess, continually takes the middle way. He advocates temperance in eating and drinking (1.263, 2.32-34), in exercise (1.277), in sleep (1.286), in pious fasting (3.393), even in the enjoyment of music and study. He regards riches as "God's good gifts, and blessings" (2.168) but satirizes the avaricious vitriolically. He himself is neither rich nor poor (1.14) and is content in his state of mediocrity (1.412). His preference for the *via media* is a matter not only of temperamental bias but also of intellectual conviction (see Chap. VI).

He never preaches abstinence. God has given men the pleasures of the world to be enjoyed. Although the Church Fathers sternly disapprove, he sees no harm in moderate love-play among young people: "to kiss coming and going . . . to talk merrily, sport, play, sing, and dance, so that it be modestly done, go to the Ale-house and Tavern together" (3.120). Although he warmly condemns the abuse, he approves the use of alcoholic drinks. Wine is "*Helen's* bowl, the sole Nectar of the Gods, or that true *Nepenthes* in *Homer*, which puts away care and grief" (2.282). He himself is a teetotaler.

He is seldom opinionated. Whatever he may believe concerning the question under discussion, he is likely to present both sides of it, sometimes so copiously that it is hard to pick out his own view. He cites opposing authorities on the issue of the reality of witchcraft (1.231, 240-41), on the influence of the stars on human destiny (1.235), on the advisability of marriage (3.284-93), on what kind of melancholic humor it is that fosters the intellectual powers (1.485-86), etc. In the field of religion—and in this field alone—he is intolerant, sometimes violently so (see Chap. VI); yet he is capable of seeing that, in the prevailing religious dissention, "there is a general fault in us all" (3.428).

Above all Burton is the humanitarian. His sympathy is continually stirred by the spectacle of wretchedness which he sees from his Minerva's tower.

This characterization of Burton is not yet complete. His studiousness and his piety will be discussed in later chapters. His credulity, his moderation, and his humanitarianism will be further elaborated.

Chapter IV: SCHOLARSHIP

FOR THIRTY YEARS, Burton writes in his fourth edition, he has been a scholar "penned up most part" in his study, and he has had the use of the excellent libraries of Oxford (Shilleto, 1.13). At some time before 1628 he became Christ Church librarian. He seems to have been on familiar terms (see 1.19n) with John Rouse, Bodleian librarian from 1620 to 1652. Before his death he had gathered a personal library of about fifteen hundred books, not a small private collection in the seventeenth century. Obviously he made good use of his opportunities for study.

Every reader of the *Anatomy* must have been impressed by the multitude of authors quoted or cited in it, and doubtless many have wondered idly just how many Burton has used. He names over thirteen hundred authors, but it is not possible to determine just how many of these he has consulted at first hand. The number of individual works to which he refers is very much greater. He was acquainted, of course, with books not mentioned in the *Anatomy*. The volumes which he bequeathed to the Bodleian and Christ Church libraries[1] include many whose titles do not appear in it. But it is a fair assumption that every work that he knew well and respected greatly has contributed something to his book.

He has "wronged no authors, but given every man his own" (1.22) in the innumerable references of text and marginalia. "I cite and quote mine Authors (which howsoever some illiterate scribblers account pedantical ... I must and will use)" (1.23). He is somewhat haphazard in carrying out this resolution. Most of his references are clear and definite enough for anyone who can expand his abbreviations (*e.g.*, "Clem. Alex. paedag. lib. 3. c. 3"). Some of them, however, lack specific book and chapter numbers, and some merely name the author ("Erasmus," "Tertul."). Many of his quotations are not identified in any way, and some of these will probably remain forever unidentified. His secondhand quotations are not always designated as such[2] with the result that he appears to have read more than he actually has. Yet there can be no doubt that he sincerely desires to avoid plagiarism.

There are numerous errors in his quotations and attributions.[3] Evidently

[1] See S. Gibson and F. R. D. Needham, "Lists of Burton's Library," *Oxford Bibliographical Society Proceedings and Papers*, I (1922-26), 222-46.

[2] Edward Bensly has done some ingenious work in identifying the immediate sources of Burton's secondhand quotations. See "Burton, Barclay and Owen," pp. 285-86; various items in *Notes and Queries*, 1903-09. Gottlieb (*Burton's Knowledge of English Poetry*) has found instances in which Burton has quoted English verse at second hand without acknowledgement of the immediate source.

[3] See Bensly, "Some Alterations and Errors," pp. 205-08.

43

he depended a great deal on memory. According to Anthony Wood, he was unsurpassed in his "dextrous interlarding" of his conversation with quotations. His memory must have been remarkably retentive. It was not retentive enough, however, to meet the demands that he made upon it as he composed the *Anatomy*.

Burton's sources are not only numerous but highly diversified. He has read whatever his manifold interests and inclinations have suggested. He is conscious of his planlessness and speaks of it with mock deprecation: perhaps because of "a running wit, an unconstant unsettled mind," he has yielded to "a great desire, (not able to attain to a superficial skill in any [subject]) to have some smattering in all." He cites Plato and Lipsius to justify his dislike of being "*a slave of one science*." He has a "roving humour," has "confusedly tumbled over divers authors in our Libraries, with small profit for want of art, order, memory, judgement" (1.14). He is not really ashamed of the diversity of his learning. In his period specialization was not yet a requisite of scholarship.

Discussion of the sources of the *Anatomy* is likely to degenerate into pointless enumeration. I shall merely name the principal fields of Burton's reading and within each a few of the authors whom he seems to have found especially informative, interesting, or inspiring, adding occasional notes concerning works which have a particular interest.

Burton's medical reading covers the greatest possible chronological range. Since he shared the respect for the wisdom of elder times which prevailed in his age, ancient and medieval works were to him as much a part of medical literature as the latest treatises. The earliest of his Greek authorities is Hippocrates; the one whom he cites most often is Galen ("the common Master of them all, from whose fountain they [all] fetch water," 2.119). Other Greek writers whom Burton cites frequently are Aretaeus, a contemporary of Galen's; Aetius, a medical compiler of the late fifth and early sixth centuries A.D.; Alexander of Tralles, sixth century.

Greek medicine was adopted, preserved, and enriched by Arabian physicians and through them reached western Europe in the eleventh century. Greco-Arabic theory still dominated medical thought in the early seventeenth century. Burton is well acquainted with the Arabians: Rhasis, Avicenna, and others of less consequence. His principal medieval European authorities are Arnold of Villanova and Bernard of Gordon.

He has consulted dozens of Renaissance medical writers. Those whose names occur most frequently are Antonius Guianerius, Fernelius (Jean François Fernel), Montanus (Johann Baptista De Monte), Lemnius (Ludwig Lemmens), Piso (Nicholas Lepois), Crato (Johann Craton von Kraftheim), Laurentius (André du Laurens), Felix Plater, Mercurialis (Geronimo Mercuriale), Hercules de Saxonia. To each of these I have found fifty or more references. Although these men were physicians of solid reputation in their day, they do not, like some of the authorities mentioned earlier, figure prominently in the annals of medicine, for they were traditionalists, not trail-blazers. Among Burton's Renaissance authorities, however, one finds a few whose fame has proved more enduring. He refers very often to Paracelsus, medical iconoclast of the early sixteenth century, and he mentions Vesalius, Fallopius, and Pareus.

In the specific field of mental diseases, Burton has made good use of treatises on melancholy by Laurentius and Hercules de Saxonia (both mentioned above) in addition to their more comprehensive works. He has drawn considerable material also from treatises on mental ills by Pratensis (Jason van der Velde), Heurnius (Jan van Heurne), Franz Hildesheim, Sckenkius (Johann Schenck), and Aelianus Montaltus (Filoteo Elião de Montalto). There are over seventy references to Montaltus' *Archipathologia* (1614) in the *Anatomy*. It is not really possible, however, to distinguish Burton's psychiatric from his medical reading. A general medical work of the Renaissance or earlier periods is more than likely to contain a psychiatric section.

A great deal of Burton's information on general psychology also comes from his medical authorities. Yet there are four works of psychological rather than medical character which should be mentioned: the treatises on the soul by Aristotle, Melanchthon, and Vives, all entitled *De Anima*, and *Turrius, sive de Intellectione Dialogus* by Girolamo Fracastoro, the Italian physician who is best known as the author of a poem on syphilis.

In the field which Burton would call natural history, Aristotle, Aelian, and Pliny are, statistically speaking, his most important sources. Ptolemy, Brahe, Kepler, and Galileo are his principal astronomical authors, although their names do not appear really frequently. I shall say more of Burton's scientific studies in a later chapter.

He is interested not only in the natural but in the supernatural. For material on spirits and black magic, he turns especially often to Johann Weier's *De Praestigiis Daemonum* (1563). Weier ("Wierus") made himself notorious in his day by opposing the traditional beliefs concerning witchcraft; but in spite of its rationalism, his book contains a great deal of lurid material about the activities of the Devil and his party. Some of Burton's other sources of information on spirits, witches, and sorcery are: *Malleus Maleficarum* (1494), by Jakob Sprenger and Heinrich Kramer, Cornelius Agrippa's *De Occulta Philosophia* (1531), Jean Bodin's *Démonomanie* (1580), Ludwig Lavater's *De Spectris* (1570), Thomas Erastus' *Repetitio Disputationis de Lamiis seu Strigibus* (1578), Strozzi Cicogna's *Magiae Omnifariae vel Potius Universae Naturae Theatrum* (1606), Jean Jacques Boissard's *De Divinatione et Magicis Praestigiis . . . Tractatus Posthumus* (?1615). He draws many of his tales of the supernatural from books dealing primarily with other subjects, works by Augustine, Ficino, Cardan, etc.

One of the most important categories in Burton's reading is the literature of religion. Few men have known the Bible better than he. He has Biblical texts ready for every conceivable occasion. His references to the Bible are incomparably more numerous than those to any other work. His favorite book evidently is the Psalms. He is thoroughly familiar with the books of wisdom: Proverbs, Ecclesiastes, the apocryphal Ecclesiasticus, Job. He refers very often to stories in Genesis, I Samuel, Matthew, and Luke. Among the prophetic books, he knows Isaiah best; among the Pauline epistles, Romans.

He is well read in the works of the Church Fathers, especially those of Augustine, Jerome, Chrysostom, and Cyprian. He refers to Augustine considerably more often than to any other theologian. He is less familiar with or less interested in the later medieval theologians. He cites Bernard of Clairvaux and Thomas Aquinas fairly often, however, and shows some knowledge of Bonaventura, Abelard, Scotus, and some others.

One would expect him to show more interest than he does in the works of the leaders of the Reformation. Their names appear in the *Anatomy* but not often. I find eleven references to Luther, only six of them to specific works, and four quotations or paraphrases of Calvin (and two indefinite references). There are a few references to works by Beza and Mornay and one to a work by Zwingli. Burton refers often to Melanchthon as a psychologist, very seldom as a theologian. He mentions Girolamo Zanchio more often than any other sixteenth century religious writer, but is more interested in Zanchio's posthumous book on divination than in his theological writings. Burton makes occasional use of works by English clergymen, especially William Perkins' *Whole Treatise of the Cases of Conscience* (1608) and John Abernethy's *Christian and Heavenly Treatise* (1615). Hooker does not appear.

Like most educated men of his period, Burton is quite at home in the moral literature of the ancient world. He quotes the ethical and philosophical writings of Plato, Aristotle, Plutarch, Seneca, Cicero, and Boethius very often.

He has absorbed the principal historical and biographical works of antiquity: notably those of Herodotus, Xenophon, Polybius, Plutarch, Livy, Tacitus, Diogenes Laertius, Lucan, Suetonius, Curtius (*De Rebus Gestis Alexandri Magni*). He draws occasionally upon Eusebius' history of the early church, Bede's ecclesiastical history, and Matthew Paris' history of England. He seems to find Renaissance chronicles less useful than those of antiquity, but he has read a number of them: Polydore Virgil's history of England, Hector Boethius' history of Scotland, Machiavelli's history of Florence, Philippe Comines' *Memoires*, William Camden's

Britannia, and others. Although he owns a copy of Holinshed's *Chronicles,* he does not refer to this work in the *Anatomy.* He has read several Renaissance biographies, for example Machiavelli's life of Cosimo di Medici and the biographies of Paulus Jovius. He uses historical and biographical works principally as sources of illustrative tales and instances.

His love of the remote, adventurous, and exotic is indicated by the number and range of the books that he has read concerning geography, travel, and strange peoples. A list of his readings in this category "would constitute a fair geographical index of his and preceding days."[4] Some of his information on these subjects comes from ancient authors: Herodotus, Strabo, Tacitus, Pausanias. But the Renaissance, the age of discovery and exploration, produced a far richer travel literature than any earlier period, and Burton has read widely in it. He remembers a great deal of detail from Marco Polo's *Travels; Africae Descriptio* by the Moorish writer Leo Africanus; books on the New World by the early sixteenth century Jesuit missionary José de Acosta; J. Aubanus Bohemus' *Omnium Gentium Mores* (1537); Sebastian Münster's *Cosmographia* (1544); *Navigationes* (1510) by Lodovico di Varthema ("Vertomannus"); *Turkish Journey* by Ogier Ghislain Busbecq ("Busbequius"), sixteenth century Flemish traveller; *Expeditio in Sinas* (1615) by Matteo Ricci ("Riccius"), celebrated Italian Jesuit missionary to China. This list could be considerably extended (see 2.103). Some English names appear among Burton's travel authors: Hakluyt, Purchas, Sandes, Moryson, Knolles.

Burton's knowledge of *belles lettres* shows that as a schoolboy he learned his classical lessons well. He is intimately acquainted with the predictable Latin authors. His quotations from Virgil (especially from the *Aeneid*), Ovid, and Horace run into the hundreds. His excerpts from the poems of Catullus, Juvenal, Martial, and Perseus and from the plays of Plautus, Terence, and Seneca are also very numerous. He refers frequently to Aulus Gellius' *Attic Nights.*

Although somewhat less impressive, his knowledge of early Greek literature is quite respectable. The Homeric epics are among his favorite books. He refers somewhat frequently to the plays of Euripides and Aristophanes, less frequently to those of Sophocles and to the fragments of Menander. (He does not seem to have read Aeschylus.) He has some acquaintanceship with the poets: Hesiod, Anacreon, Musaeus, Pindar, Theocritus.

He seems to have a taste for the works of the satirists and raconteurs (Latin and Greek) of late classical times: Petronius, Apuleius, Lucian, Athenaeus. He has read several of the romances by late Greek writers: Heliodorus, Philostratus (the *Apollonius* is romance rather than bi-

---

[4] Robert R. Cawley, *Unpathed Waters: Studies in the Influence of the Voyagers on Elizabethan Literature* (Princeton, 1940), p. 96.

ography), Achilles Tatius, Aristaenetus, and others. References to some of the romances are very numerous.

The English poet[5] whom Burton knows best and apparently likes best is Chaucer, "our English *Homer*" (3.181). He quotes frequently (in black letter) from the *Canterbury Tales*, three times from *"Chaucer's neat poem of Troilus and Cresseide"* (3.129), and once from *The Parliament of Fowles*. The Wife of Bath's cynical love-lore seems to appeal to him greatly. Spenser he regards as "our modern *Maro*" (3.34), and he quotes occasionally, sometimes at length, from *The Faerie Queene*. Drayton, apparently because he wrote a set of *Heroic Epistles*, is "our English *Ovid*" (1.299). Most of Burton's quotations from Drayton are from this work. He is well acquainted with Marlowe's and Chapman's *Hero and Leander* and with Daniel's *Complaint of Rosamond*. Among the English poets whom he quotes less frequently is Shakespeare *(Venus and Adonis* and *The Rape of Lucrece)*, "an elegant Poet of ours" (3.79).

As for Elizabethan prose works, he has at least a slight acquaintanceship with Lyly's *Euphues*, Sidney's *Arcadia*, and Joseph Hall's *Characters*. He has read Bacon's *Essays* and *New Atlantis*.

Burton recommends playgoing as a recreation for the cure of melancholy (2.91-92), but he probably does not regard the contemporary drama of the public stages as serious literature. He seems to consider Ben Jonson's plays more respectable than the rest, however, for they have serious satiric purposes and follow classical precedents. Burton's own Latin comedy, *Philosophaster*, belongs, like Jonson's plays, in the Plautine-Terentian tradition. Burton quotes from or refers to *Every Man out of His Humor*, *Volpone*, and *Epicoene*. He quotes from two of Jonson's translations of Catullus, one of which (3.274) appears in *Volpone* and the other (3.158) in *The Forest*. Jonson is "our arch poet" (3.158n).

There are many reminders in the *Anatomy* of Shakespeare's plays. Burton knows some of Shakespeare's stories from having read the sources, but references to these obviously do not mean that he has read the plays. He also repeats proverbs which appear in Shakespeare. But he shows unquestionable knowledge of Shakespeare's drama only twice: He refers to *"Benedick* and *Beatrice* in the Comedy" (3.117) and he quotes the final couplet of *Romeo and Juliet* (3.216).

Burton refers twice to Chapman's *Sir Giles Goosecap*. He borrows a translation of some verses by Anacreon (3.195) from *Technogamia*, a play by Barten Holliday, a fellow Oxfordian. This play (published 1618) was performed at Christ Church three days before *Philosophaster*. There is no

---

[5] Gottlieb's dissertation on Burton's knowledge of English poetry (see Chap. II, note 30), deals with Burton's acquaintanceship with English literature thoroughly and perhaps definitively. The dissertation includes appendices on Burton's use of English medical treatises, pious works by English clergymen, and works on spirits and witchcraft written by Englishmen.

further evidence in the *Anatomy* of knowledge of the English drama. Burton's library, however, included over seventy plays not mentioned in the *Anatomy*.

Burton is not ill acquainted with the literature of his own country. His library includes many English literary works, more than one would expect from a reading of his book. Yet the contribution which English literature has made to the *Anatomy* is incomparably smaller than that of the classical literatures. The fact that, like other Renaissance Englishmen, he praises English poets by comparing them to classical poets indicates his relative valuation.

Burton has done some reading in Italian literature. He is familiar with Castiglione's *Courtier* and Ariosto's *Orlando Furioso*. He refers infrequently to Dante's *Inferno*, Boccaccio's *Decameron*, and Petrarch's sonnets.[6] His acquaintanceship with French literature seems to be limited to Montaigne's *Essais* and Rabelais' *Gargantua* and *Pantagruel*. He has considerable enthusiasm for a Spanish play, the *Celestina* (?1499). He makes one indefinite reference to the mad Don Quixote (2.107).

The neo-Latin literature of the Renaissance has also supplied material for the *Anatomy*. Burton refers several times to a fifteenth century romance, *Euryalis and Lucretia*, by Aeneas Sylvius (Pope Pius II). He has read More's *Utopia* and various works by Erasmus. For these two authors he has a high esteem. He quotes from lyric poems by Célio Calcagnini ("Calcagninus"), Lochaeus, Angerianus, Baptista Mantuan, and George Buchanan. He is well acquainted with Joseph Hall's *Mundus Alter et Idem* (?1605) and with John Barclay's two fictional works, *Euphormionis Satyricon* (1603, 1607) and *Argenis* (1621).

None of the preceding categories in Burton's reading has been treated exhaustively. Others could be added: books on statecraft (by Plato, Aristotle, Giovanni Botero, Jean Bodin, and others), on women, on rhetoric, on agriculture, etc.

II

Burton has read Aristotle's *Poetics*, Horace's *Art of Poetry*, Scaliger's *Art of Poetry*, and other works containing critical opinion, but he is not greatly interested in literary criticism. His critical thinking is very simple, adequately expressed by a line from Horace which he uses as a motto on his engraved title page: "Omne tulit punctum, qui miscuit vtile dulci" (*Ars Poetica*, line 343). In his preface (1.18) he quotes two lines from

---

[6] Burton's acquaintanceship with Aretine's dialogues is only apparent. While he was preparing his second edition, he read Kaspar von Barth's *Pornodidascalus* (1623) under the impression that it was a Latin translation of Aretine's Italian. Actually it was a translation of a Spanish translation (by Ferdinand Xuarez) of an Italian work in the manner of Aretine. See Johannes Hoffmeister, *Kaspar von Barths Leben, Werke und Sein Deutscher Phönix* (Heidelberg, 1931), p. 39.

the same source (334, 344) which likewise express the idea that the literary artist mingles edification with pleasure.

He vindicates his treatise of love on Horatian grounds: "mine earnest intent is as much to profit as to please; *non tam ut populo placerem quam ut populum juvarem;* and these my writings, I hope, shall take like gilded pills . . . my lines shall not only recreate but rectify the mind" (3.6). He hopes to deter men from "the vanities and fopperies of this heroical or Herculean Love, and to *apply remedies unto it*" (3.8). Romances such as those of Apollonius Rhodius, Eustathius, Achilles Tatius, and Chaucer *(Troilus and Creseyde)* "are tales you will say, but they have most significant Morals, and do well express those ordinary proceedings of doting Lovers" (3.129).

When he disapproves of a book, the reason is the possible harm that it may do the reader or simply its frivolity. He warns "Inamoratoes" against reading "nothing but Play-books, idle Poems, Jests, *Amadis de Gaul, the Knight of the Sun, the Seven Champions, Palmerin de Oliva,* [Sir] *Huon of Bordeaux, &c.* Such many times prove in the end as mad as *Don Quixote*" (2.107; cf. 3.124). He considers the tastes of the English country squires contemptible: "If they read a book at any time . . . 'tis an English Chronicle, *Sir Huon of Bordeaux, Amadis de Gaul, &c.* A Play-book, or some pamphlet of News, and that at such seasons only, when they cannot stir abroad, to drive away time" (1.370). Such books he seems to regard as pleasant but not profitable. Yet he himself owned copies of plays, popular romances, jest books, reports of murders and prodigies.

III

It is easy to make lists of Burton's authorities. It is not so easy to distinguish and define the influences to which he responded.

Aside from the Bible, the book which he knows best is Virgil's *Aeneid.* From this poem he constantly draws quotations for the embellishment of his text. His mind is full of the lines, the images, the persons, and the events of the *Aeneid.* But no one would think of attempting to demonstrate a Virgilian influence upon Burton's thought or style.

Another favorite author is "that wise *Seneca*" (1.30). It could be that Seneca's essays and moral epistles have modified Burton's thinking. There is an occasional somberness in Burton's discourses on human weakness and on the nature of wisdom which might in some degree be due to his reading of Seneca. Ethical principles appear in the *Anatomy* which he might have learned from Seneca, but he might have learned them from Plato, Aristotle, Plutarch, Cicero—or from an Oxford tutor. He uses Seneca much as he uses Virgil. When a Senecan sentence comes to mind which supports or embellishes the thought which he is expressing, he inserts it. One reason for his frequent quotation of Seneca's works, both essays and plays, is the aphoristic character of Seneca's writing. For the same reason he very often quotes Cicero, Proverbs, Ecclesiastes, Job. It is conceivable that he might have used the Vedas or the Koran, if he had known them well, in much the same way, with no thought of adopting their doctrines.

St. Augustine is the religious writer whom Burton knows best and is one of the dozen writers whose names appear most often in the *Anatomy*. "Austin" is quoted, cited, or mentioned about one hundred and fifty times. Burton refers frequently to *The City of God*, the commentaries on the Psalms, and the *Confessions*, less often to about twenty other works. (Several of his quotations from Augustine are not specifically identified.) Since Augustine is Burton's principal religious authority and since religion is a principal theme of the *Anatomy*, it might be worthwhile to examine the uses that Burton makes of his works.

Burton quotes Augustine on the inanity of most literature, on the superficiality of most judgments of books, on the evils of controversy, on the frivolousness of human desires and preoccupations, on the pettiness of the causes of war, on the folly of litigation, on the corrupting effects of poetry, on the brevity and wretchedness of human life, on the evils of drink, on the misery of the schoolboy, on the possibility of justifiable suicide, on the flatness of the earth, on the pleasures and benefits of Scriptural reading, on the evils of sexual love, on the enormity of heresies and idolatries, on the hope with which God sustains us. Augustine appears frequently among Burton's authorities on the nature and activities of evil spirits. He contributes several quotations and opinions to Burton's account of the vicious effects of unregulated passions, to his consolatory discourse for the tribulations of mankind, to his general essay on love, and to his comfort for the despairing Christian.

Some of the Augustinian ideas appearing in the *Anatomy* are specifically ontological or theological. God is the source of all things (3.441). The beauty of God is superlative and ineffable (3.360, 361, 362). God is *"only good"* and no man *"can be justified in his sight"* (1.45). God directs human life in accordance with purposes not apparent to men (3.472). The soul is "a spiritual substance moving itself" (1.188); it is immortal, created of nothing, infused in the embryo (1.187). No man can be "God's friend, that is delighted with the pleasures of the world," but he that purifies his heart may see God (3.364). God's loving care is extended to every human soul (2.16); He desires and solicits our love (3.361); let man turn to God alone for help (3.492). God spares and pardons the man who does not spare himself (3.488). The only safety lies in penitence (the final lines of the *Anatomy*, (3.394).

Although a survey of this sort cannot be absolutely exhaustive, the foregoing is a reasonably complete representation of Burton's use of St. Augustine. It does not reveal a substantial Augustinianism. Many of the subjects on which Augustine is quoted or cited are miscellaneous and inconsequential. The ideas which I have called "ontological" and "theological" are commonplaces. If they originated with Augustine, they had passed into common possession long before Burton's time. There is no indication in the *Anatomy* that Burton was interested in the principal theme of *The City of God*. He seems to remember, rather, what the author has to say on the nature and powers of devils. Burton's beliefs concerning Original Sin, grace, and predestination have points in common with Augustine's, but the same points appear in the Articles of the Church of England. He does not quote Augustine on predestination.

One gets the impression that, if Burton had never read Augustine, the *Anatomy* would have been a little shorter but not significantly different. He would still have had plenty of authors to serve his purposes. Augustine appears usually in company with other authorities, sometimes several others. No one of them would be greatly missed. Burton uses Augustine —and Chrysostom, and Jerome, and Bernard—just about as he uses Virgil and Seneca; when Augustine's opinion is convenient and pertinent, he inserts it. His quotations from Augustine are likely to be epigrammatic: "Misit ad nos Epistolas et totam scripturam, quibus nobis faceret amandi desiderium" (3.361n); hope is *"vita vitae mortalis"* (3.368-69).

If likeness were a certain indication of influence, one could declare confidently that Burton owes a great debt to Erasmus. The similarities between the *Anatomy* and *The Praise of Folly* are striking. Erasmus and Burton strip the pretentious disguises from the same categories of fools with the same animated mockery. The parallels are especially close in those parts of the two books devoted to the subtle inconsequentialities of scholastic learning, to abuses in the Roman Catholic Church, and to Christian worship which observes the letter but ignores the spirit. There are perceptible but indefinite phraseological resemblances. Erasmus' *Complaint of Peace* could have inspired Burton's caustic comments on warfare among Christians. He could have learned from Erasmus' *Enchiridion* (see especiaily XIII, v) that Christianity is rather a way of life than a body of doctrine or a round of ceremonies. Unfortunately for the source-hunter, he refers to *The Praise of Folly* no more than a dozen times (comparatively not often), to *The Complaint of Peace* only twice, and to the *Enchiridion* not at all.[7] There is no very good reason to believe that Burton took anything from Erasmus beyond his acknowledged borrowings. Although he has ideas in common with Erasmus, he could have found these elsewhere or could have evolved them independently. The resemblance between them probably means no more than common mem-

---

[7] Burton refers to the *Colloquies*, to the *Epistles*, and to minor works and takes numerous proverbs from the *Adagia*. He makes several unspecific references to Erasmus.

bership in the Democritean brotherhood of derisive onlookers, to which Lucian also belongs. Erasmus, like Burton, seems to feel a kinship with Democritus and Lucian.[8]

The positive conclusion that one reaches through a study of Burton's use of his sources is that he has been influenced by too many to have been genuinely influenced by any. His mind is diversely curious, receptive, and retentive. There is nothing really distinctive about his philosophical, religious, or social opinions. He is not neo-Platonic, or Averroistic, or Thomistic. He is simply a Jacobean Englishman, an Anglican, who believes what most of his cultivated countrymen believe, although he is a little on the conservative side. His characteristic ideas come from many books—perhaps to some extent from oral discourse—, certainly not specifically from Ecclesiastes, or Jerome, or Boethius, or Macrobius, or Bodin, or J. C. Scaliger, or Lipsius. He might have drawn his ideas concerning the curative power of gems or the social wisdom of the Chinese from this or that individual author, but it is not possible to trace his views on more general and significant questions to specific sources.

Investigation of Burton's sources yields little than Burton himself has not revealed. One is likely to accomplish no more than the compilation of lists.

There is the possibility of stylistic influences. It could be that the Hippocratic Democritus, Lucian, and Erasmus have affected Burton's manner of writing. If so, the influence is very subtle, more a matter of scoffing lightness of tone than of specific characteristics of syntax or phrasing. Burton himself defends his plainness, looseness, and informality by referring to the precept and practice of Seneca (1.31). His style, however, does not resemble Seneca's closely. It is Senecan in the sense that it exemplifies various "Senecan" stylistic traits which were fashionable in the early seventeenth century. "Burton runs the full gamut of Senecan style, to which he adds his own exuberant amplification."[9]

IV

Burton feels that he "must apologize" for the fact that the *Anatomy* is a vernacular work: "it was not mine intent to prostitute my muse in *English,* or to divulge *secreta Minervae,* but to have exposed this more contract in *Latin,* if I could have got it printed." But the "mercenary Stationers" would have nothing to do with a Latin work (1.28-29). Did Burton consult with a stationer before beginning the *Anatomy?* Was he told that a Latin work would be inacceptable, and did he therefore choose

[8] Concerning Democritus, see *The Praise of Folly,* tr. Dean, pp. 37, 64, 88. Erasmus translated twenty-eight of the dialogues of Lucian.

It is unlikely that the Rabelaisian element which some readers have perceived in the *Anatomy* is due to discipleship, conscious or unconscious. Burton praises Rabelais as "that French *Lucian*" (1.262) but reveals no great familiarity with his works. His references to Rabelais are very few.

[9] Williamson, *The Senecan Amble,* p. 200. (See Chap. I, note 9.)

to write in English? Or did he go to a publisher with a Latin manuscript in some stage of completion and, because of the publisher's objection or rejection, translate it into less "contract" English? Neither of these suppositions seems in the least likely. Burton is probably not being altogether candid. One learns from this passage at least that Burton, like many other Renaissance scholars, affects a condescension toward his mother tongue.

His Latin comedy shows that he did not lack the ability to make the calamitous mistake that he suggests. He probably could have written the *Anatomy* as readily in Latin as in English. Certain brief portions actually are in Latin. In each case there is an obvious reason, usually the salaciousness of the subject matter. ("Good Master Schoolmaster, do not English this," 1.244n.) Burton seems to share the widespread and curious belief that obscenity is less harmful to the learned than to the laity. His longest Latin passage, however, is an acrimonious complaint concerning the abuses in the English universities and the Anglican Church (1.374-78). He is here addressing himself specifically to university men and clerics. The message is not intended for readers with small knowledge of Latin.

Very often he shows consideration for his less learned readers by translating his Latin quotations. His translations tend to be highly approximate, "sometimes rather paraphrases than interpretations" (1.32), and are often incomplete. They are sometimes briefer and more pungently phrased than their originals.

Burton has much Latin but considerably less Greek. He seems to have read his Greek authors in Latin translation when he could. He customarily quotes Greek works from Latin translations. "*Greek* authors, *Plato, Plutarch, Athenaeus,* &c. I have cited out of their interpreters, because the original was not so ready" (1.32). But surely Greek texts of Plato, Plutarch, and many other standard Greek authors were readily available at Oxford. There are a few Greek quotations in the *Anatomy,* for example three excerpts from the Greek original of Hesiod (but Burton more often quotes Hesiod in Latin). There are six Greek titles in Burton's library.

Burton seems to have known some Italian. He quotes two unidentified lines of Italian verse (3.322). He consistently, however, uses Harington's English translation of Ariosto's *Orlando Furioso,* Robert Tofte's English translation of Varchi's *Blazon of Jealousy,* and a Latin translation of Castiglione's *Courtier.* Apparently he could read French. He seems to have read Jacques Ferrand's *Erotomania* between 1628 and 1632, at which time it was available only in French. The copy in his library is in French. Yet he uses Latin translations of works written in French by Comines, Bodin, and others. He uses Barth's Latin translation of the Spanish play *Celestina.*

Burton is really bilingual. His mastery of Greek, Italian, and French does not seem to have been very sure. There is no substantial evidence that he knew Spanish or German.[10] He is conscious of the pleasure which the study of languages affords, "Hebrew, Greek, Syriack, Chaldee, Arabick, &c." (2.102), but he does not seem to have indulged in these pleasures very much. The fact that he never travelled would have limited his linguistic accomplishments.

v

Burton's abundant display of his learning shows that he is proud of it. His assiduity in study shows that he has enjoyed the acquiring of it. He warmly recommends the pleasures of study (in moderation) as a cure for melancholy: "what a world of Books offers itself, in all subjects, arts, and sciences, to the sweet content and capacity of the Reader! In *Arithmetick, Geometry, Perspective, Opticks, Astronomy, Architecture, Sculptura, Pictura* . . . What vast Tomes are extant in *Law, Physick, & Divinity*, for profit, pleasure, practice, speculation, in verse or prose, &c.! . . . he is a very block that is affected with none of them" (2.102). There follows enthusiastic discussion of the delights and rewards of various specific fields of learning. In successive editions of the *Anatomy*, Burton expands the passage on the pleasures of study (2.100-12) to nearly two and one-half times its original length.

In Burton's eyes there is great merit, dignity, and desert in learning: "not one of a many proves to be a scholar, all are not capable and docile, *ex omni ligno non fit Mercurius*. . . . Kings can invest Knights and Barons . . . Universities can give Degrees . . . but he, nor they, nor all the world, can give Learning, make Philosophers, Artists, Orators, Poets . . . Learning is not so quickly got . . . few can compass it" (1.354-55). He values his academic calling and his membership in the Oxford community.[11] Oxford, he says, is a "learned and noble . . . society . . . a royal and ample foundation" (1.14). With evident pleasure he quotes an exclamation which King James is said to have made upon visiting Oxford in 1605: "If I were not a King, I would be an University man" (2.105). He refers to Oxford and Cambridge as "our most flourishing Universities, which produce in abundance men most learned in every branch of learning, and men to be respected for every kind of virtue" (1.379).[12] Christ Church is "the most

[10] His library includes a copy of *Underricht der Hoch Teutschen Sprache* by A. Oelinger (1574).

[11] According to Murry ("Burton's 'Anatomy,'" p. 39) and Evans (*Psychiatry of Robert Burton*, pp. 7-8, 15), Burton disliked university life intensely and held his fellow scholars in contempt. I cannot agree. There is no doubt that Burton felt at times that at Oxford he was leading a drab existence, isolated from the world of action and events, yet clearly he found compensations in academic life. Without question he was contemptuous of pedants, blockheads, and venial academic time-servers. So are we all.

[12] This is Shilleto's translation of Burton's Latin.

55

flourishing College of *Europe*" (1.13). He has high regard also for those who aid and encourage learning, "munificent *Ptolemies,* bountiful *Maecenases,* heroical Patrons, divine spirits" (2.106). He specifically mentions Sir Thomas Bodley and others.

The labor required of scholars is long and painful. "It may be, their temperature will not endure it" (1.355). The world gives the scholar little esteem and less wealth. The abuses in the universities and in the church are unquestionably serious. Yet Burton has not lost faith in the compensations and values of learning.

If he could reorder society as he saw fit, he would place capable scholars in the posts of responsibility in church and state—offices commonly held by unqualified favorites, sycophants, and politicians—so that their knowledge and wisdom might be at the service of the commonwealth. In his utopia "Rectors of Benefices [are] to be chosen out of the Universities, examined and approved, as the *Literati* in *China. . . .* If it were possible, I would have such Priests as should imitate *Christ . . .*" (1.115). No man would be "eligible, or capable of magistracies, honours, offices" unless he were "sufficiently qualified for learning, manners, and that by the strict approbation of deputed examinators: first Scholars to take place, then Soldiers" (1.116). Burton does not think of humane scholarship as merely an acquirement which enables its possessor to train others to be humane scholars so that these in turn may train others. He held the characteristic Renaissance belief that the function of scholarship is service to the state. The learned constitute society's most valuable class.

The *Anatomy* itself illustrates Burton's belief in the practical value of scholarship. Excluded from positions of political and ecclesiastical authority in which he might put his accomplishments and acquirements to use in the direction of public affairs, the scholar may at least offer his services to his fellow men through his writings. This is precisely what Burton, lacking more effective means of serving society, has done. Penned up in his study, he has absorbed the wisdom of the ages from many books. He has winnowed out the best that has been thought and said (his winnowing is, to be sure, very imperfect) and has presented his knowledge and his wisdom in a form which was particularly palatable to his generation.

The *Anatomy* is a work of scholarship. One finds in it information and opinion which the author has assembled from the works of many others. There is no pretense of originality. Although the book as a whole is highly original, the author claims merely that "the method only is mine own . . . we can say nothing but what hath been said, the composition and method is ours only, & shows a Scholar" (1.23). Burton seems to have no ambition to be an original thinker, an intellectual leader. But there is pride in his claim to scholarship. This quotation is less modest than might be apparent to many twentieth century readers.

Chapter V: SCIENCE

THE ANATOMY OF MELANCHOLY is purportedly a scientific work. It contains a much smaller proportion of medical and psychological material than its title seems to promise. Yet the parts of it devoted to psychopathology and closely related subjects remain a principal element in it, and it contains a good deal of scientific lore in other fields. It is appropriate certainly to discuss Burton as a scientist. How scientific is he? What is the nature of his scientific thought, and what is its relation to the scientific developments of his period?

This inquiry will require some characterization of the two kinds of scientific thinking which, as historians of science have frequently pointed out, were in competition in sixteenth and seventeenth century Europe. There was a traditional science, a heritage from the middle ages and the ancient world, whose authority was rapidly declining. There was also a new science, a consequence of the Renaissance revival of interest in the physical world and in man as a physical and temporal creature. This was modern science in its infancy. Before it lay a future of astonishing development and influence. It has, in fact, made the world over.

These two patterns of scientific thinking are confusedly entangled with each other in the scientific literature of the Renaissance. Although there are many writers who seem unaffected by the new ideas, there are none, even among the most progressive, who have achieved complete independence of tradition. It is necessary for the sake of clarity, however, to discuss the old and new sciences as if they were mutually exclusive schools of thought.

The conservative scientific scholar did not pursue the truth concerning the world and physical man through observation and experiment. He was inclined to believe that the truth, in so far as it was any proper concern of man's, had already been ascertained and recorded. He sought it therefore in the Scriptures and in the writings of the great thinkers of the past: Aristotle, Plato, Galen, Pliny, Avicenna, Averroes, Aquinas. He had a respect for the works of early writers which was sometimes veneration. In general, the earlier the writer, the greater his respect. Because of his high regard for his predecessors, he perpetuated and defended ancient errors.

The scientific writer of this category is never at ease without the support of authority. The margins of sixteenth century medical works bristle with references to the respected writers of the recent and remote past. Medical debate is likely to consist simply of appeals to authority. The author may sometimes question a statement of Aristotle or Avicenna; more often he attempts to explain in what sense a dubious opinion is to be understood, how it may be true.

The respect for ancient authority which appears so often in Renaissance scientific thought—and for that matter in all intellectual fields during the Renaissance—was related to and doubtless in some measure due to the wide currency and obstinate persistence of the medieval idea of the decay of the world. According to this view, the world and man were created perfect. The Original Sin was followed by a sudden decline to a less perfect state, and all of subsequent history is a story of further, though slower, degeneration. In the early days the flora and fauna of the earth were more vigorous, more beautiful, more amiable than they are now. Men were taller, stronger, longer-lived (*e.g.*, Methuselah), and they possessed mental abilities corresponding with their physical superiorities. But the world has sadly worsened, and with it men's bodies and minds. The world is, indeed, suffering from the degenerative infirmities of senility. It will shortly die. The end will come in about the year 2000.

A belief in the superior mental capabilities of men living in earlier and happier epochs naturally leads to respect for their opinions. How could one hope to be wiser or to perceive the truth more clearly than Macrobius or Boethius or Lucretius, who lived several centuries earlier than oneself? Aristotle, who lived some centuries nearer the original perfection than these, would correspondingly surpass them in wisdom and perception. For a man of the later ages it would be futile to emulate or to attempt correction of the earlier authors. He must be content to learn from them.

There was further discouragement to intellectual venturesomeness in the idea that God had imposed limits upon human knowledge, which only the presumptuous would seek to violate.

The older science, then, was traditional, authoritarian, deductive, static. Because of its basic assumptions, it could not hope greatly to extend the boundaries of human knowledge or to make any significant modification of ideas already formulated. The function of the scientific writer was simply exposition and, when authorities disagreed, harmonization. Whereas the scientist of the new school looked forward to indefinite extension of man's understanding of his environment and to continually greater mastery of it, the scientist of the old school looked backward to happier days which could never return.

The traditional science was not really a science at all in the modern sense of the word. To us the word *science* implies an experimental and inductive study of nature which is systematic and highly exact. It implies continual growth and modification, continual extension of accepted knowledges, continual progress toward a goal which continually recedes. The branches of Renaissance learning which dealt with physical nature had no such characteristics. We call them sciences for lack of a better word, and in discussing them we often allow the modern connotations of *science* to obscure their true nature. We need another term. The Renaissance, incidentally, used *science* as a term for all branches of learning. Most of the particular studies concerned with physical nature fell into the categories known as *natural history* and *natural philosophy*.

The new science of the Renaissance is distinguished by a curiosity and an intellectual independence like those of the pre-Socratic Greeks. Its exponents turned from books to nature itself. Its accomplishment lay more in the development of a method and in the defining of an attitude than in actual scientific discovery. The method was that of observation and experiment, of careful and systematic collection of data, of inductive reasoning on the basis of such data. It was, in short, our "scientific method." The attitude was one of confidence—a confidence in the power of the human mind to discover the principles governing the multifarious forms of nature, a confidence in God's approval of such researches, a confidence also in the possibility of improving the physical conditions of human life through the application of scientific knowledge. This confidence was belief in progress—that is, in the possibility of progressively greater understanding of nature, of progressively greater power in the hands of men, of forms of human living progressively less laborious and more comfortable.

In seventeenth century England, this method and this attitude were especially associated with the name of Sir Francis Bacon, whose service to the new movement lay in his giving verbal form to them, in acting as spokesman and standard bearer. In two of his works especially, *The Advancement of Learning* (1605) and the *Novum Organum* (1620), he gave the new ideas eloquent and convincing expression, and these two volumes served as a nuclear point around which, during the two following generations, the new movement crystallized.

Although in Burton's day most of its great achievements lay still in the future, the new science nevertheless could claim substantial accomplishment in at least a few fields. With Arabic mathematics to build on, Renaissance mathematicians had made considerable progress. Anatomy had become a science in the modern sense. Astronomy had advanced somewhat spectacularly. In 1543 Copernicus had published the hypothesis of the heliocentric planetary system, which he had developed from the conjectures of certain ancient cosmologists. By the time of the publication of Burton's *Anatomy*, this hypothesis had been corrected and greatly strengthened by the observations and conclusions of Tycho Brahe, Kepler, and Galileo. Astronomy offered more significant and more profound modifications in man's conception of the physical universe than any other science. Its hypotheses, moreover, were arresting and imaginatively appealing, and their significance should have been obvious even to the most thoughtless. Among the more thoughtful they were the subject of intense concern and voluminous debate.

A seventeenth century seeker of information would be likely to find, in the literature of any science, a perplexing confusion of the old and the new. If like Robert Burton he had an inquisitive and receptive mind, he would be inclined to accept the new; if like Burton he felt the respect for authority which was general among the learned, he would be disinclined to reject the old.

II

Burton knew at least a little about most of the sciences and a great deal about some of them. I shall discuss his knowledge of specific scientific fields,[1] beginning with astronomy, or cosmology, the science which, next to psychiatry, seems most to have engaged his interest. He was acquainted with the traditional Ptolemaic conception of the universe, with the new Copernican idea of the sun-centered planetary system, and with sundry theories which lay somewhere in between.

The Ptolemaic system, as it was known to the Renaissance, represents the universe (or "world") as earth-centered and therefore man-centered. The earth is a solid, stationary sphere surrounded by ten hollow, concentric revolving spheres, all but the outer one transparent. Between the earth and the innermost of these (the first heaven) is the region of air and, beyond that, the region (or sphere) of fire. The moon moves about the earth in the innermost of the celestial spheres, Venus in the next, Mercury in the third, the sun, Mars, Jupiter, and Saturn respectively in the next four. The eighth sphere, called the firmament, is the region of the fixed stars. Then comes a crystalline, or watery sphere (the waters above the firmament), and finally a solid, opaque shell which incloses the entire universe. By divine decree this opaque tenth sphere, the *primum mobile*, turns unceasingly with enormous velocity, and through imparting its own motion to all the heavens within, it provides the motive power of the whole system. Probably most Renaissance Englishmen thought of the spheres as solid crystalline surfaces to which the various heavenly bodies were attached, and probably most of them credited the Pythagorean idea that their motion produced an exquisitely beautiful music audible only to the most sensitive and perceptive. Some Renaissance writers, however, represent the spheres as intangible and penetrable (see *Anatomy*, 2.57).

Although the foregoing statement may fairly represent the Elizabethan layman's idea of the heavens, the Ptolemaic system is really much more

[1] I have found information concerning various fields, authors, and specific works mentioned in the following pages in vols. V-VIII of Lynn Thorndike's *History of Magic and Experimental Science* (New York, 1923-58). Paul H. Kocher, in *Science and Religion in Elizabethan England* (San Marino, Cal., 1953), deals capably with several of the ideas and movements discussed in this chapter.

complex than it has suggested. In order to make theory fit the observed movements of the planets—at the same time preserving the inviolable principle of circularity—it was necessary to introduce certain assumptions: the assumption of the eccentric orbit, *i.e.*, a circular orbit within which the earth stood off center; the assumption of the epicyclic orbit, *i.e.*, a small circular orbit whose center moved along a large circular orbit around the earth. Epicycles were imposed upon epicycles. Ptolemaic astronomy was geometrically and mathematically very abstruse. Those who are in a position to know assure us that the system, to a surprising degree, meets the requirements of such astronomical facts as can be observed without a telescope.

The heliocentric theory proposed by Copernicus and later defended, corrected, and strengthened by Kepler and Galileo, was recommended by its relative simplicity and by experimental verification.[2] But to be accepted it had to overcome the stubborn inertia of the human mind. Not only were there warm defenders of the Ptolemaic astronomy but also theorists who, reluctant to accept anything quite so revolutionary and so contrary to Scripture as the Copernican system, proposed various compromise hypotheses. The most notable of these was the theory of the eminent Tycho Brahe, predecessor and teacher of Kepler, according to which the sun, moon, and fixed stars revolved around the earth, the other five planets around the sun (see 3.138). Another compromise was that of Origanus (*Ephemerides*, 1599, 1609), who proposed that the earth, at the center of the universe, had a diurnal motion but no annual motion. Burton seems to find this theory reasonable (2.61).

Although English astronomical opinion was highly confused in the earlier seventeenth century, England had rather definitely decided against Ptolemy. "The rapid decline in England of the Aristotelio-Ptolemaic astronomy is attested by almost every discussion of the science of the heavens" written after 1600, even those in theological works and "cheap popular handbooks." Copernicus, Tycho, Gilbert, and Galileo "become the authorities cited, instead of Aristotle, Ptolemy, and the Arab astronomers."[3] During the years when Burton was composing the *Anatomy*, the Ptolemaic astronomy was regarded—at least by those with valid claims to astronomical expertness—as an error of the scientific past.

Burton adopts the new without giving up the old.[4] His ancient authorities include astronomers and cosmologists of widely divergent opinions, not only Aristotle and Ptolemy, but Pythagoras, Leucippus, Democritus,

[2] In Burton's time the principal remaining objection was the fact that no stellar parallax had been observed.

[3] Francis R. Johnson, *Astronomical Thought in Renaissance England* (Baltimore, 1937), p. 249. See also p. 292.

[4] Robert M. Browne, in "Robert Burton and the New Cosmology," *Modern Language Quarterly*, XIII (1952), 131-48, deals with Burton's cosmological thinking in detail with especial attention to the "Digression of the Air." He shows that Burton was remarkably well read in the field and that he was capable of intelligent criticism

Epicurus, Aristarchus of Samos (who propounded a heliocentric theory in the third century B. C.), and others. (Of necessity he knows the opinions of some of these only as they are recorded by later classical writers.) He seems to have little acquaintanceship with medieval astronomical writers (*e.g.*, Alfraganus and Sacrobosco), but he has thoroughly explored the astronomical literature of the Renaissance.

Most of the astronomical treatises which he has read are, in fact, sixteenth and seventeenth century works. Evidently he continued to read in the recent astronomical literature throughout his life, for in each successive edition of the *Anatomy*, new authorities appear, some of them of very late date. In the final edition there is citation of John Wilkins' *Discovery of a World in the Moon*, 1638, which advances some rather bold conjectures concerning the habitability of other worlds than ours. Burton owned more than twenty books on astronomy,[5] including Copernicus' *De Revolutionibus Orbis* (edition of 1543) and Wilkins' *Discovery*. In astronomy and in the related fields of mathematics and magnetism, Burton kept well abreast of current theory.

Evidence of his interest in novel astronomical theories appears on the first page of the preface in the first edition of the *Anatomy*.[6] Here he refers to the heliocentric theory and to the hypothesis of plural worlds. Most of the cosmological material in the *Anatomy*, however, is concentrated in the "Digression of the Air" (2.40 ff.). Here the rival theories, presented without perceptible organization, contradict and neutralize one another. Burton is keenly interested in all of them and seems reluctant to relinquish any of them altogether. Apparently he rejects the crystalline sphere (between the firmament and the *primum mobile*) and the sphere of fire (between the terrestrial air and the lunar sphere). He is incredulous concerning eccentrics and epicycles and is rather appalled by the speed which the assumptions of the older astronomy require of the outer spheres in their revolutions around the earth. He is excited by the idea of plurality of worlds, or infinitude of worlds (see especially 2.62-64). He refers often to his prototype Democritus and to Giordano Bruno as supporters of this

---

of the various hypotheses. He finds that Burton read a great deal of astronomical literature between 1621 and 1638 and that his additions in successive versions increase the length of the "Digression of the Air" by "some fifty percent" (p. 131). He discovers, however, no definable change of opinion on astronomical questions. Burton was "an alert, inquisitive man" who knew "few of the answers but all of the questions" (p. 145).

[5] Browne, p. 145. "Johnson's list of English astronomical works between 1500 and 1645 includes works by only four important writers neither mentioned by Burton nor represented in his library" (pp. 145-46).

[6] A passage in *Philosophaster* also reveals this interest (ed. Jordan-Smith, p. 81). It seems more likely that Burton wrote the passage in 1605, when he first composed the play, than that he added it in revising. The astronomical works of the authors mentioned were all published before 1600.

hypothesis. The "green children" who, according to Nubrigensis, fell from heaven might have come from another planet (2.62). He is somewhat troubled by the thought that, if there are races on other planets, terrestrial man is not, as he has supposed, unique and pre-eminent in God's creation ("where's our glory?" 1.344). Burton is, in fact, quite aware of the difficult philosophical and theological problems which the theory of plurality raises (2.64). He is interested in the recently discovered moons of the planets (see especially 2.62) and in Galileo's telescope (see 2.110). "Some of [the moons] above Jupiter I have seen myself by the help of a glass eight feet long" (2.62n). His study of astronomy seems to have involved more actual observation than his study of physiology.

Although Burton leans slightly to Origanus' theory, no really definite opinion takes shape in his discourse on astronomy. It seems unlikely that he seriously believes in the Ptolemaic concept of the world, yet he never really repudiates it. It is not possible to state his cosmological opinions.

At the close of his discourse on astronomy, Burton seems to yield up cosmological questions, not quite in despair, but with a feeling that no answer is possible and that none is really needed. The multiplication of theories arouses his derision. He associates astronomical speculations with the questions in divinity which overcurious theologasters presumptuously raise. The answers to these, perhaps also to astronomical mysteries, God will reveal when He "sees his time" (2.69). Like his younger contemporary Milton, Burton is strongly attracted by the cosmological theorizing of his period, and like Milton he finally turns from it in the conviction that for man the truth is incomprehensible and superfluous. The happy man is he who is not troubled over "what comets or new stars signify, whether the earth stand or move, there be a new world in the Moon, or infinite worlds, &c." (2.177).

His familiarity with novel ideas concerning the structure of the heavens and the disposition of the stars did not affect Burton's adherence to the ancient science of astrology. He was, says Anthony Wood, "a curious calculator of nativities." Although the *Anatomy* contains less astrological lore than Wood's statement might lead one to expect, the subject appears fairly frequently. Burton condemns "Divinators" (1.420) and quack "Astrologers" (3.149), but there is no real question in his mind that the stars, exerting their virtue upon the humors, influence human temperament (see 1.456-57, 3.64-65) and therefore human destiny. He is himself a Saturnist (1.14) and is consequently inclined to melancholy. Various bits of astrological information, supported by such authorities as Paracelsus, Cardan, Pontanus, Ficino, appear in his discussions of the causes and cures of melancholy. He counsels consulting an astrologer in choosing a wife, at least in cases of extreme doubt (3.356-57).

At the time when the *Anatomy* was published, the validity of astrology had been a subject of sharp disagreement among the learned for over a century.[7] Burton has read the arguments of both the attackers and the defenders of astrology (1.235-37, 2.17). He rather firmly takes his stand with the moderate proponents. Astrology is definitely useful, perhaps necessary, in the practice of medicine. As for philosophical and ethical implications, he declines to follow those astrologers who deny the freedom of the will: the stars "do incline, but not compel; no necessity at all, *agunt non cogunt*: and so gently incline, that a wise man may resist them . . . they rule us, but God rules them" (1.235; *cf.* 3.279). The story that Wood has preserved concerning Burton's suicide is obviously nonsense. A man who believed that the stars did no more than gently incline would neither predict the date of his own death nor hang himself to prove the infallibility of astrological prediction.

The references to alchemy in the *Anatomy* are rather few and reveal only a vague knowledge of the subject. Many of them are derisive. Burton sometimes includes alchemists in his lists of quacks and imposters.[8] In a passage on the vanity of learning, he represents the alchemist as a deluded fool: he "spends his fortunes to find out the Philosopher's stone forsooth, cure all diseases, make men long-lived, victorious, fortunate, invisible, and beggars himself, misled by those seducing imposters . . . to make gold" (1.422). He quotes Felix Plater: "all Alchemists are mad, out of their wits" (1.133). Yet he writes that "our Alchemists . . . and Rosy-Cross men . . . can make gold, separate and alter metals, extract oils, salts, lees . . ." and mentions other wonders (2.110-11). He includes alchemists among those who are to be given a place in the colleges of his utopia, "Not to make gold, but for matters of physick" (1.111n). The most famous of the later alchemists was Paracelsus, Swiss physician and natural philosopher of the early sixteenth century. Burton does not hesitate to cite Paracelsus as a medical authority and refers to works by several of his disciples.

The sixteenth century alchemists were more than would-be transmuters. Paracelsus himself was less interested in gold-making than in searching out the recondite basic principles of nature.[9] The discovery of new medi-

---

[7] See Don Cameron Allen, *The Star-Crossed Renaissance* (Durham, N. C., 1941). Allen refers specifically to Burton's opinions, pp. 153-54. See also Kocher, *Science and Religion*, pp. 201-24.

[8] In *Philosophaster* an alchemical pretender (who is also a Paracelsan physician) inveigles large sums from a nobleman by promising to produce the philosopher's stone for him (ed. Jordan-Smith, pp. 119, 135-37, 153). The swindler's victim has dreams of wealth, power, and luxury (pp. 137-39) much like those of Sir Epicure Mammon in Jonson's *Alchemist*. Indeed the resemblances to Jonson's comedy are striking. In his prologue Burton emphatically makes the point that his play is eleven years old (p. 19), probably to anticipate suspicions of plagiarism.

[9] See F. Sherwood Taylor, *The Alchemists* (New York, 1949), pp. 195 ff.; Henry M. Pachter, *Paracelsus: Magic into Science* (New York, 1951), pp. 111-20 *et passim*.

cines, he believed, should be among the primary objectives of alchemy. He was a laboratory experimenter and a loud-mouthed oppugner of authority. Because of his posthumous fame and influence, alchemy and "chemical" medicine became virtually identified with Paracelsism in the later sixteenth century. He and his party are said to have developed laboratory techniques indispensable to the more scientific chemistry of later times.

Although Burton's knowledge of Paracelsan chemistry is largely pharmacological, his reading in the works of Paracelsus and his followers has, at all events, given him some contact with the rudimentary chemistry of his day. He shows a slight knowledge also of Andreas Libavius' *Alchemia* (1597), a book of practical character regarded as the soundest chemical treatise of the sixteenth century.

If one looks for Burton's conception of matter, he finds simply the traditional idea of the four elements, to which the four humors of the human body are analogous (1.170). He is acquainted with the Democritean atomic theory of matter, which had some Renaissance adherents, and with Paracelsus' theory of the three hypostatical principles inherent in matter, "*sal, sulphur, mercury*" (2.56); but he does not seem to find these doctrines convincing.

He has some miscellaneous information in the field of physics. His study of recent astronomical literature must have acquainted him with the laws of motion as they were understood after Kepler. He has done some reading in the literature of optics (1.180, 2.110), though he says little on this subject. He seems to be interested in magnetism and the compass, for he has read treatises in this field by William Gilbert (*De Magnete*, 1600), Martin Ridley (*Treatise of Magnetic Bodies*, 1613), and Niccolo Cabeo (*Philosophia Magnetica*, 1629).

He writes with enthusiasm of mathematical and geometrical studies (see 2.109-12). It is evident that he has followed the new developments in mathematics, for he recommends "*Napier's Logarithms* [and] those tables of artificial *Sines* and *Tangents,* not long since set out by" his former fellow student and good friend Edmund Gunter (2.111). John Napier was the discoverer of logarithms. His treatise on the subject, which Burton mentions in his first edition, appeared in 1619. Gunter's *Description of the Sector*, first mentioned in Burton's second edition, was published in 1620.[10] According to Wood, Burton "was an exact Mathematician . . . [and] understood the surveying of lands well."[11] There is no occasion for display of mathematical proficiency, however, in the *Anatomy.*

Burton's biology consists principally of fanciful misinformation: "As I

[10] Burton dates Napier's book 1620, Gunter's 1623. He owned two copies of Gunter's book.
[11] *Athenae Oxonienses,* ed. Bliss, II, 652.

go by *Madagascar,* I would see that great Bird *Ruck,* that can carry a Man and Horse or an Elephant, with that *Arabian Phoenix* described by *Adricomius;* see the Pelicans of *Egypt,* those *Scythian* Gryphes in *Asia . . ."* (2.42). He refers to the basilisk, the voice of the mandrake, the ichneunon's destruction of the crocodile, the royal chivalry of the lion, the loves of the plants, etc. Pliny, Aelian, and Herodotus are the immediate or ultimate sources of many of his notions. But he has read also biological studies of recent date, some of them by pioneers in the field: *e.g.* in zoology, Gesner, Aldrovandi, Belon, Rondolet; in botany, Leonard Fuchs ("Fuchius"), L'Obel ("Lobelius"), Mattioli, and Bauhin.[12] His copy of Gerard's *Herbal* is mentioned as a special bequest in his will. The pictures and exact descriptions which he has found in Renaissance biological works please him greatly (2.103). Accurate woodcuts and detailed descriptions were new developments in biology.

Geography and cartography should perhaps be included among Burton's sciences. He knows a great deal about these subjects (see especially 2.41 ff., 103). Although he often cites ancient authors, *e.g.* Strabo and Herodotus, he is well aware of the sixteenth century revolution in geography. He finds great pleasure in studying the maps and treatises of the men who effected this revolution, notably Mercator, Hondius (who edited and completed the work of Mercator), Ortelius, and Münster. The latest work in this field that I have found in the *Anatomy* is Nathaniel Carpenter's *Geography* (1625).[13]

The *Anatomy* includes brief discourses on physiognomy, chiromancy (palmistry), and metoposcopy (character reading from the markings on the forehead) as means of detecting melancholic inclinations (1.238-39). The author defends these sciences, in which he has done some reading, from the ridicule which they seem to have drawn upon themselves.

III

The brief survey in Chapter IV of Burton's reading in the medical sciences indicates the traditional character of his information and of his thinking in this area. Hippocrates, Galen, Avicenna, and Bernard of Gordon are among the authorities whom he quotes most often. With some exceptions, his Renaissance authorities are traditionalists, Galenists. Like Burton, they refer often to the ancient writers, from whom they have derived their medical principles.

[12] He knows Fuchs better as a physician than as a botanist; Mattioli better as a pharmaceutical authority than as a botanist. Gesner's more significant botanical studies were not published until the eighteenth century.

[13] This work contains a reference to the *Anatomy,* perhaps the earliest (see Jordan-Smith, *Bibliographia Burtoniana,* p. 74). Its author was a fellow of Exeter College, Oxford, and possibly an acquaintance of Burton's. The *Geography* was published by Cripps, publisher of the *Anatomy.* It includes some anti-Ptolemaic astronomical theory. Burton refers to it only once (2.43).

SCIENCE

At first glance, the exceptions suggest that Burton might not be a medical fundamentalist after all. Historians of science[14] seem generally agreed that the most important of the medical pioneers of the sixteenth and early seventeenth centuries were Girolamo Fracastoro, Paracelsus, Andreas Vesalius, Hieronymus Fabricius, Ambrose Paré, and William Harvey. The names of all of these but the last appear in the *Anatomy*. Before concluding that Burton was receptive to new medical ideas, however, one should know more about his acquaintanceship with the medical innovators.

Fracastoro's principal contributions to medical science were a poem on syphilis and a treatise on contagions. Burton refers frequently to Fracastoro's not very novel psychological treatise (*Turrius, sive de Intellectione Dialogus*, 1555) but shows no interest in his ideas on contagious diseases.

Paracelsus was the outstanding exponent of the new "chemical" theory of healing (iatrochemistry), which, in the late sixteenth and early seventeenth centuries, was in sharp conflict with the traditional Galenic medicine. The latter is based upon the physiology which assumes the existence of the four humors. "*Paracelsus* wholly rejects and derides this division of four humours and complexions" (1.197). (Actually Paracelsus does not consistently reject the theory of the humors.) The Galenist explains all disease as humoral abnormality. His therapy consists in ridding the body of the offending humor by phlebotomy or purgation or in counteracting its effect by application of its opposite (cold cures a hot disease, moisture corrects dryness, etc.). Paracelsus denies the efficacy of these undiscriminating methods and seeks a specific remedy for the specific disease. He applies like to like, the likeness consisting of affinity indicated by sometimes esoteric "signatures." Instead of the organic medicines of the Galenist, he prescribes chemical remedies prepared in the laboratory by processes supposed to extract from the raw material its healing virtue, its pure spirit.

To the modern mind, Paracelsus' theories seem just as fantastic as those of the Galenists. He is a significant figure in the history of medicine, however, because he sought to learn the healing art by laboratory experiment rather than by the reading of authoritative books and because his precept and example encouraged others to do likewise. The arrogant vigor of his attacks on Galenism, moreover, greatly weakened the authority of medical tradition. Paracelsus bragged that "he did more famous cures by [his methods] than all the *Galenists* in *Europe*" and called "himself a Monarch [;] *Galen, Hippocrates*, infants, illiterate, &c." (2.278). In 1527

[14] E. g. Fielding H. Garrison, *An Introduction to the History of Medicine* (Philadelphia and London, 1922); Arturo Castiglione, *A History of Medicine* (New York, 1947); A. Wolf, *A History of Science, Technology, and Philosophy in the 16th & 17th Centuries* (London, 1950); Thorndike, *History of Magic and Science*.

he dramatized his campaign against medical orthodoxy by a public burning of Avicenna's *Canon*. By 1600 he had won a large and highly vocal posthumous following.[15]

The name of Paracelsus appears more than fifty times in the *Anatomy*. Yet Burton does not altogether approve of him. His satiric treatment of alchemists applies to Paracelsus as well as to others. In an outburst against medical imposters, he names "Paracelsians" among other types (1.360).[16] Paracelsus goes too far, he implies, in insisting that to cure melancholy a physician must be "a Magician, a Chemist, a Philosopher, an Astrologer" and in limiting physic to "chemical medicines" (2.17). He is acquainted with several of the attacks on Paracelsus and his theories, notably Thomas Erastus' *De Medicina Nova* (1572). Characteristically, however, he declines to take sides in the Paracelsan-Galenic controversy: "let them agree as they will, I proceed" (2.279).

Burton seems to have read or consulted about ten of Paracelsus' numerous works and shows real familiarity with two of these: *De Zilphis et Pygmaeis* and *De Morbis Amentium*.[17] His references to Paracelsus indicate that his attitude toward him is not altogether sceptical and certainly not contemptuous. He refers several times to works by two later iatrochemical physicians, Crollius and Quercetan, whom he seems to regard as dependable authorities, and shows slighter knowledge of works by other Paracelsans. His inclusion of alchemists among the physicians of his utopia shows that he believes that the Paracelsans have something of value to contribute. Burton does not dismiss Paracelsism—or any other body of doctrine—, but he is not a Paracelsan. Indeed he shows little familiarity with the details of Paracelsan theory.

Andreas Vesalius is the most celebrated of the sixteenth century anatomists. By his careful dissections and exact observations, he did more perhaps than any other man to make anatomy a modern science. The most notable of his successors were Hieronymus Fabricius, known especially for his study of the valves in the veins, and Fabricius' pupil William Harvey.[18] In the early seventeenth century, the new anatomy led to Harvey's theory of the circulation of the blood and thus to the discrediting of the theory of the four humors and of the Galenic medicine

[15] In England Paracelsism was received cautiously but not altogether hostilely. See Paul H. Kocher, "Paracelsan Medicine in England: The First Thirty Years (ca. 1570-1600)," *Journal of the History of Medicine*, II (1947), 451-80.

[16] The quack doctor of *Philosophaster* (see above, note 8) professes himself a disciple of Paracelsus (ed. Jordan-Smith, p. 33), and there is some Paracelsan jargon in the play (pp. 27, 73).

[17] These are both available in English translation in *Four Treatises of . . . Paracelsus*, ed. Henry E. Sigerist (Baltimore, 1941).

[18] Two other sixteenth century anatomists of high accomplishment were Eustachius, rival of Vesalius, and Falopius, Vesalius' pupil and supporter. Burton seems to know a pharmaceutical work by Falopius. He does not name Eustachius.

in general. Burton refers to Vesalius as an expert anatomist (1.134) and repeats the slanderous rumor that, to observe the functioning of the arteries, he "was wont to cut up men alive" (1.171). There is no good reason to believe that he had read Vesalius' celebrated work, *De Fabrica Humani Corporis* (1543). He refers his reader to Fabricius' *De Loquela Animalium* (1603) for information on the jealousy of dogs (3.301) but shows no knowledge of Fabricius' work in anatomy. He does not refer to Harvey at all. Harvey's *De Motu Cordis* (1628) came too late for Burton's first three editions but not for the fourth.

Paré appears once in Burton's book, cited with other authorities on a point concerning the hymen (3.326). Paré's more significant work concerns military surgery.

In spite of some acquaintanceship with the works of medical liberals, Burton's medical thinking remained solidly Galenic. There was, however, no urgent reason why he should incorporate the recent improvements upon or deviations from Galen in the *Anatomy*. Paracelsan medicine was justifiably suspect. Fracastoro's work on contagious diseases, Paré's ideas on the treatment of gunshot wounds, and the discoveries of Vesalius and Fabricius concerning the heart and veins had no direct bearing on Burton's psychiatric problems. Harvey's *De Motu Cordis* was not published until 1628, and its revolutionary significance would not have been immediately evident.

Burton cannot be accused, moreover, of neglecting recent medical literature. He makes use of several (conventional) books of very late date. These include treatises within his specific field: Franciscus Hildesheim, *De Cerebri et Capitis Morbis Internis Spicilegia*, 1612; Aelianus Montaltus, *Archipathologia*, 1614; Hercules de Saxonia, *Tractatus de Melancholia*, 1620. A Jacobean seeking the latest opinions in the field of psychiatry would turn to such works as these. There was no "new psychiatry."[19]

IV

Earlier generations than Burton's had, scientifically and intellectually speaking, looked backward. Later generations have looked forward. Burton lived and wrote a book purportedly scientific in a period when some men were looking backward, some forward. In which direction did Burton face?

[19] Modern scholars have pointed out—and perhaps exaggerated—the scientific rationality of the psychiatric thinking of Paracelsus and Johann Weier (see Pachter, *Paracelsus*, pp. 227-38; Gregory Zilboorg, *The Medical Man and the Witch During the Renaissance*, Baltimore, 1935). But these men, however enlightened they may have been, did not propose anything sufficiently original, comprehensive, and systematic to be called a new psychiatry. Burton, in any case, was well acquainted with Paracelsus' *De Morbis Amentium* (published posthumously in 1567) and Weier's *De Praestigiis Daemonum* (1563).

The two foregoing sections should have made it clear that he was not the obstinate traditionalist that his constant citation of ancient and medieval writers might make him appear. He had read works by many of the men who stand out in histories of science as contributors to progress in their respective fields. The important names in Renaissance astronomy are Copernicus, Brahe, Bruno, Kepler, and Galileo. Burton knew works by Brahe, Kepler, and Galileo very well and had at least some acquaintance with Copernicus and Bruno. In spite of his respect for Ptolemy and Aristotle, he was not reluctant to accept revision of the Ptolemaic world. He was very well informed on recent developments in mathematics, magnetism, and geography. He knew something about the novel chemistry of the Paracelsans and was acquainted with works by some of the leaders in the biological sciences. Although he evidently had no appreciation of the revolutionary developments in anatomy, he had done considerable reading in late medical works.

In the period when "up-to-date" first had a meaning and when keeping up was first becoming a virtue, Burton was not altogether behind the times. He probably knew more about the recent scientific discoveries than his great progressive contemporary Francis Bacon.

The mere presence of the pioneer names in the *Anatomy*, however, does not mean that the author has adopted the new ways of thinking or that he has rejected the traditional sources. In his mind, good books do not become outdated. In most scientific fields, the Renaissance pioneers are very much in the minority among Burton's authorities, and to most of them, individually considered, his references are infrequent. Their appearance in the *Anatomy* shows that Burton's curiosity has prompted him to read widely and diversely and suggests that he might be conscious of exciting new developments in scientific fields. Obviously he is fully conscious of such developments in, for example, astronomy.

His methods of acquiring and presenting knowledge concerning nature and physical man are the old methods. One learns from books. In every field there is a literature from which one may learn, and the older works in the field deserve particular respect. In expounding scientific material one cites the authors from whom he has drawn in order to validate his own treatise. Indeed the *Anatomy*, with its margins crowded with notes, is an extreme example of the authoritarian method of composition. Without adopting their manner of thinking, Burton has added the works of the "neotericks" to his body of authoritative literature. Kepler and Ptolemy, Paracelsus and Galen stand side by side as authorities. Considerable confusion arises from the association of such irreconcilable thinkers.

One would expect an early Stuart Englishman who was interested in the sciences to show some familiarity with the scientific writings of Sir Francis Bacon. Burton seems to admire Bacon. He cites Bacon's *Essays* several times. In connection with his own utopia, he twice mentions *The New Atlantis* (in the third and later editions of the *Anatomy*) among other utopian works, but he says nothing of its content. He refers also to Bacon's *De Vita et Morte*. Although he had several years to do so before the publication of his first edition, however, Burton apparently never read *The Advancement of Learning*. Since the *Novum Organum* appeared only one year before the *Anatomy*, one would hardly expect to find reference to it in Burton's first edition, but he could have given it a place in his second edition, or his third, or fourth. If he ever read it, he shows no evidence of interest in it. His indifference to Bacon's ideas concerning the methods, functions, and potentialities of science indicate that he was not altogether alive to what was going on intellectually, that he was isolated from or indifferent to the scientific circles of his day. The Baconian doctrines were very live issues during Burton's later years. In the midst of the most stimulating and significant intellectual movement since the Reformation, he was simply unaware.

Burton takes no clear stand on the question of the decay of the world and the related question of the possibility of progress. He quotes Lipsius (but not Bacon) in opposition to the theory of decay, apparently with approval: "As arts and sciences, so Physick is still perfected amongst the rest. *Horae Musarum nutrices*, and experience teacheth us every day many things which our predecessors knew not of. Nature is not effete . . . she is still the same, and not old or consumed" (2.258). Yet he says that there are more diseases now than in olden times (1.157). He gives the opinion held by some scholars that, because of celestial changes, "the virtue . . . of all the vegetals is decayed, men grow less, &c." (2.54). He quotes Paul of Aegina (seventh century) to the effect that nothing is "*unknown or omitted*" (1.18). In these later, degenerate days, what function might a medical writer have? "Though there were many Giants of old in Physick and Philosophy, yet I say with *Didacas Stella, A dwarf standing on the shoulders of a Giant may see farther than a Giant himself*" (1.23). Burton probably does not know what he thinks about these matters. But clearly he has not caught the fever of Baconian progressivism.

Although there is some evidence in the *Anatomy* of sympathy with scientific experimentation, Burton does not understand the fundamental importance of the experimental method. There is no evidence in the *Anatomy* that Burton himself ever conducted an experiment. In one significant respect he fails to carry out his imitation of his prototype: Hippocrates found Democritus of Abdera with a book on his knee dissecting animals; Burton has the book on his knee, but he dissects no animals. He sometimes records his observations of human behavior, but these are such as any alert and thoughtful person might make, not planned and controlled scientific observations. There is no evidence that he ever actually witnessed the treatment of a demented person. There is no mention even of any phychiatric case which he has personally observed except his own, and he never refers specifically to his own symptoms or to any treatment which he personally has found helpful. Apparently it never occurs to him that firsthand observation and experience might be necessary to scientific competence. He seems to have no feeling that he has omitted anything essential.

Burton lacks not only the experimental curiosity but also the critical scepticism which the true scientific thinker must have. There were men of Burton's generation and earlier who were capable of rational examination of traditional beliefs. There was, for example, a handful of writers who questioned the current ideas concerning witchcraft.[20] Burton knows their works (see 1.231, 240-41), yet he subscribes to the irrational opinions of the majority. He knows the arguments of the authorities, classical and Renaissance, who deny the existence of evil spirits (1.206). He himself occasionally takes a stand against this or that specific notion concerning spirits (1.211, 213, 227), but he does not doubt their existence. He can reject a popular belief which is unsupported by learned authority: he does not believe that there is an ominous significance "if a hare cross the way at our going forth, or a mouse gnaw our clothes: if they bleed three drops at nose, the salt falls towards them, a black spot appear in their nails, &c." (1.418). At one time he was sceptical of his mother's remedy for ague, an amulet consisting "of a Spider in a nut-shell lapped in silk . . . *Quid aranea cum febre?*" But when he "found this very medicine in *Dioscorides*, approved by *Matthiolus*, repeated by *Aldrovandus*," he changed his mind, especially since he "saw it in some parties answer to experience."[21] He insists nevertheless that there is no efficacy in "medicines . . . that consist of words, characters, spells, and charms." These he associates with the Devil (2.290).

He is much more inclined to believe than to doubt. He repeats from a great variety of sources curious instances of the nature and activity of spirits (1.205-30), of the evil powers of witches (1.231-34), of the machinations of the Devil, of strange legendary beasts, of the loves of plants (3.16, 46-47), of the influence upon the unborn child of things seen by the mother (1.246, 293), etc. He would not have seemed unusually naïve, perhaps, to his contemporaries; yet, after all allowances for the fact that he lived in the seventeenth century, he still seems credulous.

Burton's *Anatomy* contains a great deal of information about the ideas which our ancestors held concerning the natural world and the physical nature of man. It is interesting to historians of science, but it had no

[20] See Thorndike, *History of Magic and Science*, VI, 515 ff.; Kocher, *Science and Religion*, pp. 127-33.
[21] This change of opinion occurred between the first and second editions of the *Anatomy*.

genuine scientific value even in the writer's own time. In spite of his somewhat haphazard knowledge of the new discoveries, Burton was essentially conservative, authoritarian, and backward-looking. Conservatism is not a reprehensible intellectual trait. But it is not a characteristic which inspires confidence in a man's thinking in the field of science.

To say that Burton's medicine and psychiatry were behind the times would be inaccurate. His medical ideas were those held by most physicians of his time, and there was no better psychiatry than Burton's. Yet medically and psychiatrically, the *Anatomy* has little to offer that a medieval treatise might not offer.

Sir William Osler's often quoted opinion that the *Anatomy* is the greatest "medical treatise . . . [ever] written by a layman"[22] is misleading in its implications. The statement, I believe, is quite true, but the greatness of the *Anatomy* does not lie in its medical content. It is not a milestone in the progress of abnormal psychology. Nor is it a book abounding in clinical wisdom. In its more strictly psychiatric sections, one reads of normal and corrupted forms of blood, choler, phlegm, and black bile; vapors which rise from the viscera to the cells of the brain, where they discolor the images flitting through the imagination; therapeutic procedures such as bloodlettings and purges to evacuate noxious humors; dietary directions which classify foods as hot, cold, moist, and dry in various degrees; pharmaceutical directions which are complex, fulsome, and unconvincing. The best that can be said for the *Anatomy* as a therapeutic work is that its discredited medical practices are considerably qualified by the author's humanity and common sense.

v

The Renaissance learned from the Middle Ages that curiosity was a sin.[23] As the word is commonly used in Renaissance documents, *curiosity* means a presumptuous inquisitiveness, a craving to learn what the human mind is not capable of understanding, an ambition to master God's

[22] "Robert Burton: The Man, His Book, His Library," *Oxford Bibliographical Society Proceedings and Papers*, I (1922-26), p. 183. Bergen Evans' *Psychiatry of Robert Burton* is largely devoted to the thesis that Burton is a wise and instinctively sound psychiatrist. Burton undoubtedly has a great deal of common sense and humanity, but these are hardly enough to compensate for the basic errors of his humoral physiology and psychology.

[23] Howard Schultz, in *Milton and Forbidden Knowledge* (New York, 1955), presents an illuminating study of the anti-intellectualism of the Renaissance, that is, of its condemnations of "the bifurcated sin of dubious speculation (curosity) on the one hand and corrupted learning (vain philosophy) on the other" (p. 3). Kocher discusses the concept of curiosity as it affected the English attitude toward the sciences (*Science and Religion*, pp. 63-73).

Burton, says Schultz, was "perhaps the century's best authority on curiosity of any kind" (p. 105). In the *Anatomy* the term *curiosity* refers loosely to either branch of the bifurcated sin. Burton's ideas concerning "vain philosophy" will appear in Chap. VII.

secrets. It is a form of intellectual pride. Adam, in eating of the fruit of the Tree of Knowledge, was guilty of various sins, among them curiosity (see *Anatomy*, 1.150). Scientific research and speculation naturally were sometimes condemned as curiosity. Being a seventeenth century divine and being greatly interested in the sciences, Burton must have given at least a little thought to the question of whether or not scientific study was morally defensible.

His attitude toward the search for new scientific truth is on the whole approving. He seems to take the side of the scientists in their difficulties with the clergy: Some writers "freely speak, mutter, and would persuade the world (as *Marinus Marcenus* complains) that our modern Divines are too severe and rigid against Mathematicians [astronomers?], ignorant and peevish in not admitting their true demonstrations and certain observations" (2.64). He warmly commends the botanical gardens recently established in Padua, Nüremberg, Leyden, Montpelier, "and ours in *Oxford* now in *fieri* . . . at the cost and charges of the Right Honourable the Lord *Danvers*, Earl of *Danby*" (2.247).[24] Burton's utopia will have "colleges of mathematicians, musicians, and actors . . . alchemists, physicians, artists, and philosophers; that all arts and sciences may sooner be perfected & better learned" (1.111). Every man who "invents anything for publick good in any Art or Science . . . shall be accordingly enriched, honoured, and preferred" (1.117). The provision for the advancement of the sciences and crafts is not so systematic and elaborate as Bacon's, but the intention is similar.

Yet Burton is not a wholehearted partisan of science. Among the tribulations of humanity is "*Curiosity*, that irksome, that tyrannizing care, *nimia sollicitudo, superfluous industry about unprofitable things and their qualities*, as *Thomas* defines it: an itching humour . . . to know that secret which should not be known, to eat of the forbidden fruit. . . . For what matter is it for us to know how high the *Pleiades* are, how far distant *Perseus* and *Cassiopea* from us, how deep the sea, &c? We are neither wiser, as he [Eusebius] follows it, nor modester, nor better, nor richer, nor stronger, for the knowledge of it. *Quod supra nos nihil ad nos.* I may say the same of . . . Astology . . . Magick . . . Physick . . . Alchemy . . ." (1.420-21). The effect of this passage, which comes from Burton's review of the causes of melancholy, is somewhat neutralized by the enthusiasm with which he later recommends the study of scientific subjects (in moderation) as a cure for melancholy. One finds less disputable evidence of his opinion at the close of his discussion of the various astronomical

---

[24] Gardens for botanical study had been established at various continental universities during the century preceding the publication of the *Anatomy*. See Garrison, *History of Medicine*, p. 231. The foundation stone of the Oxford botanical garden was laid July 25, 1621. See Mallet, *History of Oxford*, II, 245. Burton's reference to the construction of the garden occurs in his first edition.

theories. The cosmological theorizer, he says, merely adds to confusion: "as a tinker stops one hole and makes two, he . . . reforms some, and mars all. In the mean time the World is tossed in a blanket amongst them, they hoise the Earth up and down like a ball, make it stand and go at their pleasures" (2.66). Burton is inclined to approve the decision of Jupiter, in Lucian's *Icaromenippus*, to destroy all philosophers and "make an end of all these curious controversies" (2.67).

"But why should the Sun and Moon be angry, or take exceptions at Mathematicians and Philosophers, when as the like measure is offered unto God himself by a company of Theologasters?" (2.67). This leads into a condemnation of speculation concerning the nature of God and the workings of His mind. The attitude toward the astronomers is derisive; their endeavors are absurdly futile. The attitude toward the "Theologasters" is indignant; they are guilty not only of folly but of sin.

But it is not possible that the writer of a work on a scientific subject could be wholly dubious of the value of science. Where would Burton draw the line between defensible and indefensible scientific study? He never draws it for us, but it is not hard to see what distinction he would make. Cosmology, alchemy, and to some extent astrology, however interesting they may be, are finally futile and frustrating. But Burton never shows any doubts concerning the value of the applied sciences: metallurgy, agriculture, navigational mathematics. These contribute to the well-being of man. Medical science is justifiable because it relieves the physical sufferings of man. Psychology relieves his mental miseries and furthermore has ethical value in that it teaches man to know himself and to exercise rational self-control.

Burton's norm for the judgment of science, then, is the same as Milton's, the norm of usefulness (*Paradise Lost*, VIII, 167-78). Every body of knowledge is to be approved which has either practical or moral value. But Burton is dubious, though not altogether condemnatory, in his attitude toward those sciences which are more remote from human needs.

VI

Even apart from its outdated scientific content, the *Anatomy* is very unlike the scientific books of our own time, including those written, like the *Anatomy*, for the lay reader. There has been a considerable change in what readers expect in scientific writing, and this change began in Burton's own century.

The *Anatomy* differs markedly from modern works in the way in which it is written. The modern scientific writer sticks to his subject and is inclined to interpret its limits rather narrowly. Burton interprets his subject very broadly, follows all its possible ramifications, and often digresses widely and pleasantly. The modern scientific work, even the

75

"popular" work, is somewhat economical and severe in style. The writer's primary stylistic aims are lucidity and exactitude. Whether he knows it or not, he submits to the principles of style which Bishop Sprat laid down for the Royal Society in the 1660's. He avoids the decorative flourish and the emotionally suggestive phrase. Burton and other Renaissance scientific writers know nothing of such restrictions.[25] They freely employ the elegant embellishment, the rhetorical device, emotionally weighted diction. They often write familiarly in the first person. They seem highly tautological. Most of them write no better than their modern counterparts, possibly worse. At any rate they write differently, and the difference lies principally in their conscious striving to write with rhetorical color.

If any scientist of Burton's period could be expected to write severely, it would be William Harvey. Yet the following appears in *De Motu Cordis:* The motion of the blood

may be called circular in the way that Aristotle says air and rain follow the circular motion of the stars. The moist earth warmed by the sun gives off vapors, which, rising, are condensed to fall again moistening the earth. By this means things grow. . . .

So the heart is the center of life, the sun of the Microcosm, as the sun itself might be called the heart of the world. The blood is moved, invigorated, and kept from decaying by the power and pulse of the heart. It is the intimate shrine whose function is the nourishing and warming of the whole body, the basis and source of all life.[26]

If he had lived somewhat later, Burton would have felt constrained to stay within the limits of his subject strictly interpreted. The *Anatomy* would have been merely a treatise on a mental disease which was ill understood and which the writer was ill qualified to write on. It could never have grown and ramified, as it did, into a critique of human behavior. If Burton had observed Bishop Sprat's stylistic injunctions, if he had avoided all "luxury and redundance of speech" and written with "mathematical plainness," he would have been a very dull writer. A work like the *Anatomy* could not have been written in any later generation than Burton's.

In its fundamental objectives, also, the *Anatomy* differs widely from the modern scientific work. In our own day the scientific writer seeks simply to inform. Since modern science is supposedly amoral, he seldom

[25] Science "had not yet become a profession sharply distinguished from other professions . . . the Elizabethan natural philosopher . . . [might] be described as merely man thinking about nature—man capable of assuming other postures," Kocher, *Science and Religion*, pp. 115-16.

[26] *Exercitatio Anatomica de Motu Cordis et Sanguinis in Animalibus*, tr. Chauncey D. Leake (Springfield, Ill., 1928), pp. 70-71. There are many passages of this character in the treatises on melancholy by Bright and Du Laurens (see Chap. I, notes 13 and 15). One finds embellished and emotionally colored writing also in works not intended for the layman.

concerns himself with ethical values. When he does so, he consciously abandons his role as scientist. The Renaissance writer recognizes no sharp distinction between natural and moral philosophy and is very likely to offer moral wisdom along with factual knowledge.

The Renaissance had little regard for knowledge which had no usefulness. The desire to know simply for the sake of knowing was "curiosity." The knowledge of greatest worth and dignity was that which served a religious or moral purpose. Science was valued principally, therefore, for its religious and ethical services.[27] Its highest functions were the strengthening of men's belief and the rectification of their conduct.

To convince the reader of the value of their works, the authors of the dietaries and popular medical books of the period continually remind him that a healthy body is prerequisite to a wholesome and right-thinking mind. In expounding sciences of less obviously purposeful nature, writers justify them on the ground that they reveal in earthly and celestial nature unending evidence of the power and glory of God and of the unquestionable rightness and harmonious regularity of the world which, in His goodness, He has created for the benefit of man. Francis Bacon prays that God may "graciously grant to us to write an apocalypse or true vision of the footsteps of the Creator imprinted on his creatures."[28] There "are two Books from whence I collect my Divinity," Sir Thomas Browne writes in defending his interest in science; "besides that written one of God, another of his servant Nature, that universal and publick Manuscript, that lies expans'd unto the Eyes of all."[29]

No class of scientific writers was more conscious of the moral functions of science than the psychologists. Their books offer instruction on the interrelated physical and mental natures of man, not because the facts are interesting, but because self-knowledge is necessary to self-control and to virtuous conduct. The psychological literature constitutes the most complete and emphatic statement that we have of the ethical view of life normal among thoughtful Englishmen. It was a principal source from which they drew their ethical ideas. Several psychological treatises were available to Englishmen of Burton's generation in their own language, among them: Thomas Rogers' *Anatomie of the Minde* (1576), Thomas Wright's *Passions of the Minde* (1601), Thomas Walkington's *Optick Glasse of Humors* (1607), Pierre Charron's *Of Wisdome* (English translation published c. 1606), F. N. Coeffeteau's *Table of Humane Passions* (translation published 1621), Edward Reynolds' *Treatise of the Passions and Faculties of the Soule of Man* (1640). The authors of all of these were clergymen.

[27] See Kocher, pp. 3-28, 41-44, 151-52, 155-56, 171.
[28] *The Great Instauration, Works*, ed. Spedding, Ellis, and Heath (London, 1857-1874), IV, 33.
[29] *Religio Medici, Works*, ed. Keynes, I, 21.

The *Anatomy* belongs loosely in the category of such treatises, though it is by no means a typical member. Its purported subject is narrower than theirs; it actually covers a much greater range of subject matter than they do. Yet it offers moral instruction in psychological terms, and like the typical psychology, it is basically not a scientific, but a moral work.

Its emphasis on pathology and therapy does not make it less so. Psychiatry also has its moral usefulness. The physician Timothy Bright, in another book on melancholy, declares that the highest function of the medical profession is to correct "the infirmities of the mind. For the instrument of reason, the braine, being either not of well tempered substance: or disordered in his parts: all exercise of wisedome is hindred . . . there vnconsiderate iudgement, simplicitie, & foolishnes make their seat, and as it were dispossessing reason . . . [debase human nature] farre vnder the condition of brute beasts."[30] It is quite appropriate, says Burton, that a minister should write on melancholy: "It is a disease of the soul on which I am to treat, and as much appertaining to a Divine as to a Physician; and who knows not what an agreement there is betwixt these two professions? . . . one amends *animam per corpus*, the other *corpus per animam*" (1.36).

The moral bias of the *Anatomy* might seem to the modern reader out of place in a work purportedly scientific. In the eyes of the author and of his contemporaries, it was the ethical element which justified the book. Although its clinical usefulness may be questionable, there is permanent worth in the ethical principles which it expounds and in its moral criticism of human behavior. For this reason among others, the *Anatomy* does not, like later scientific works, lose its meaning with the passing of the years.

---

[30] *Treatise of Melancholie*, letter of dedication. Bright gave up medicine to enter the ministry.

Chapter VI: ETHICS, SOCIAL THEORY, METAPHYSICS, RELIGION

BURTON's ethical ideas come from the moral writings of the ancient philosophers and from the Gospels. The principles from these two sources are, of course, by no means irreconcilable. In fact the classical principles had long been incorporated in Christian doctrine. Neither his classical nor his Christian ethics distinguishes Burton at all from his contemporaries. All seventeenth century Englishmen were Christians. All educated Englishmen had, like Burton, read and learned to admire Aristotle, Cicero, Seneca, Plutarch, and other classical moralists.

The premise of the classical ethics is the familiar principle that reason ("right reason") will always, if it is not prevented or perverted by passion, dictate the course of virtue, the course which leads to that contentment of spirit which is the *summmum bonum* of earthly existence. Emotion, if it gains ascendancy over reason, impels man into folly, evil, and misery.

In the Renaissance psychologies, including the *Anatomy*, one finds definition and characterization of the subdivisions of the human soul and of their various faculties. There is the rational soul, the ego, which distinguishes man from beast. The rational soul is man's immortal part. Next in the order of dignity is the sensitive soul, which beasts as well as men possess and which has the faculties of sensation, motion, and emotion. Finally there is the vegetable soul, to be found in men, beasts, and plants, which in general directs the humbler physiological processes below the level of consciousness.

Renaissance psychologists and moralists devote much of their space (as various titles indicate) to the passions, faculties of the sensitive soul, because in them lie man's greatest weakness and greatest moral danger. Since the sin of Adam, the passions have been, not the obedient servants of reason that they should be, but rebellious subjects, always ready to rise in insurrection, to blind, to vitiate, or simply to overpower the rational faculties. Thus the moral problem of man is presented as an internal conflict between the rational and sensitive natures, between the human and bestial elements in man, between spirit and flesh. Since the passions are in some degree due to physical causes, there are physiological means of regulating them, for example, diet. But the remedies on which every man must finally rely are moral: unremitting vigilance on the part of the reason and unremitting effort on the part of the reasonable will.

The primary means to virtue is self-control. The prerequisite of self-control is self-knowledge. These are the motivating beliefs which pro-

79

duced the Elizabethan literature on theoretical psychology. Throughout this literature one finds echoes of the classical exhortation "nosce teip-sum."[1] The attitude of the writers is not that of the dispassionate teacher but that of the preacher.

The passions very often prove too strong for the degenerate human reason. Most men, says Burton, "suffer themselves wholly to be led by sense . . . bad by nature, worse by art, discipline, custom, education, and a perverse will of their own . . . this stubborn will of ours perverts judgement, which sees and knows what should and ought to be done, and yet will not do it." Slaves to their appetites, men "precipitate and plunge themselves into a labyrinth of cares." Because they yield to their passions, "they are torn in pieces, as *Actaeon* was with his dogs, and crucify their own souls" (1.297-98). There are, to be sure, "Some few discreet men . . . that can govern themselves, and curb in these inordinate affections, by religion, philosophy, and such divine precepts, of meekness, patience, and the like" (1.297). They presumably achieve the quietude of mind which is the *"voluptas,* or *summum bonum,* of *Epicurus, non dolere, curis vacare, animo tranquillo esse,* not to grieve, but to want cares, and have a quiet soul . . . the only pleasure of the World, as *Seneca* truly recites his opinion" (2.117-18). Such men are very rare.

Inordinate, insubordinate passion is a major cause of melancholy. With this justification Burton includes in his discourse on the causes of melancholy a somewhat lengthy treatise of the passions. In the volume on the cure of melancholy, he writes a subsection on "Perturbations of the mind rectified" (2.117-25) and a long "Consolatory Digression containing the Remedies of all manner of Discontents" (2.145-218). But Burton's concern with the passions is not to be explained altogether by their connection with melancholy. It is basically due to the dismay which he feels as he witnesses the folly, evil, and misery of human life. These, he believes, are caused by man's unreasonableness, by man's failure to rule his bestial nature.

Burton is not a Stoic. He agrees with St. Augustine that both the concupiscible and the irascible appetites are good *"if they be moderate: both pernicious if they be exhorbitant"* (1.324). God has given man passions for a purpose. Presumably lack of or feebleness of emotion would, like excess, be evil, but since passionate mankind seldom suffers from defect, moralists have little to say about it. Moderation in all things is a recurrent lesson in the *Anatomy.* The way of reason is the Aristotelian *via media.*

Expressed in Christian terms, the functions of the reason are to know

---

[1] See *Anatomy,* 1.115, 168; 2.235. The Renaissance did not usually understand the phrase in the sense in which the Greeks had used it. To the Greeks it meant "learn humility." See H. D. F. Kitto, *The Greeks* (Pelican Books, 1951), p. 111.

God and perceive His goodness, to determine His will, and to devise and direct action in conformity to it. If it is not overpowered or vitiated by passion, the Christian man's intellect, since it enjoys the benefit of divine revelation, will assuredly perform these functions. I shall discuss Burton's understanding of the will of God in a later section.

II

In his thinking concerning human society,[2] Burton extends the principle of the rule of reason from individual to social application. *Sapientia* becomes *prudentia*.

He starts from assumptions which a great many of his contemporaries would have approved: the social *summum bonum* is a condition of harmony and stability; this is to be achieved by a hierarchical social structure analogous to the pyramidal pattern according to which God has ordered all creation[3]: "God hath appointed this inequality of States, orders and degrees, a subordination, as in all other things. The earth yields nourishment to vegetals, sensible creatures feed on vegetals, both are substitutes to reasonable souls, and men are subject amongst themselves, and all to higher powers: so God would have it" (2.196). Again: "as we do reverence our masters, so do our masters their superiors: Gentlemen serve Nobles, and Nobles [are] subordinate to Kings . . . Princes themselves are God's servants" (2.199). It is right and proper that there should be a social class structure, degrees of power and dignity supported by appropriate wealth, with the king at the apex of the hierarchy. Sedition and rebellion against the existing order are unreasonable and contemptible (see 1.91-92, 3.485).

Burton believes in the superior hereditary endowment of the aristocracy. No man of mean extraction can successfully assume the manner of the born aristocrat (2.166). After pointing out some of the shortcomings of the higher classes, he assures his reader: "I do much respect and honour true Gentry and Nobility; I was born of worshipful parents myself, in an ancient family, but I am a younger brother" (2.165). He refers with great respect to the patrons who have befriended him and to the noble benefactors of Oxford. King James was "our *Amulet*, our Sun, our sole comfort and refuge, our *Ptolemy*, our common *Maecenas*, *Jacobus munificus*, *Jacobus pacificus*, *mysta Musarum*, *Rex Platonicus*[4]

---

[2] There are two competent studies of Burton's social thought: Mueller's *Anatomy of Robert Burton's England* and Patrick's "Robert Burton's Utopianism." The treatment which follows is less detailed than these and differs from them somewhat in its points of emphasis.

[3] See E. M. W. Tillyard, *Shakespeare's History Plays* (New York 1947), pp. 10-20 *et passim*.

[4] Burton here echoes the title of Isaac Wake's *Rex Platonicus* (1607), an account of King James' visit to Oxford in 1605.

. . . But he is now gone, the Sun of ours set, and yet no night follows. . . . We have such another in his room" (1.369-70; cf. 3.299-300).[5]

Fourteen pages of Burton's preface are devoted to the description of an ideal state. With apologetic facetiousness, he assumes the role of beneficent tyrant and creates on paper "an *Utopia* of mine own, a new *Atlantis*, a poetical Commonwealth" (1.109), in which reason and the will of God prevail. "If it were possible, I would have such Priests as should imitate *Christ*, charitable Lawyers should love their neighbors as themselves, temperate and modest Physicians, Politicians contemn the world, Philosophers should know themselves, Noblemen live honestly, Tradesmen leave lying and cozening, Magistrates corruption, &c." (1.115). The author believes that many of the ills of England—and therefore much of its melancholy—arise from social and economic evils[6] and that wisdom could correct them. He offers his utopia as a cure for melancholy.

It is designed to eliminate those evils, principally economic, which are responsible for the miseries which he sees around him. The changes which he would like to make are not at all radical. The existing hierarchical social order of England is to Burton right in theory. The problem, then, is to make those changes in things as they are which will actually make of England the commonwealth which she theoretically is. It is a matter of eliminating and preventing abuses—of reforming, not remaking England. Burton's "Utopia is simply an improved version of England," "a mercantilistic state with a highly developed industry and commerce, yet without the attendant evils of the complex capitalistic system which makes such development possible."[7]

Burton's ideal state is to be governed by men of proper rank, by "several orders, degrees of nobility, and those hereditary" (1.113). Lesser officials shall be responsible to "higher officers and governors of each city, which shall not be poor tradesmen, and mean artificers, but noblemen and gentlemen" (1.112). The church is organized hierarchically. Presumably a strong monarch caps the social and political pyramid.

Yet Burton's belief in the inherent superiority of the hereditary upper classes and in the propriety of submission to them is not quite firm. He writes that "*Utopian* parity is a kind of government to be wished for rather than effected" (1.113). It is odd that he dismisses the idea of "parity" because he considers it impractical rather than wrong in principle. In his utopia there will be some offices and dignities which "shall be given to the worthiest & best deserving both in war and peace, as a reward of

[5] The reference to King Charles was added in the third edition. This is Burton's only mention of him. There is reference to Prince Henry's death in Burton's first edition (Shilleto, 1.416).

[6] Mueller, pp. 35-44, shows a relation between Burton's proposed reforms and the actual economic problems of Jacobean England.

[7] Mueller, pp. 34, 62. Cf. Patrick, p. 356.

their worth and good service." He hates laws "which exclude plebeians from honours, be they never so wise, rich, virtuous, valiant, and well qualified . . . this is *naturae bellum inferre*, odious to God and men" (1.114). In his consolation for baseness of birth, he praises the practice of Switzerland, the United Provinces, and China of choosing men for high office according to learning and wisdom rather than rank (2.161-62). "How much better is it to be born of mean parentage, and to excel in worth, to be morally noble" than to possess "that natural nobility." It is better "to be learned, honest, discreet, well qualified" than to belong to a degenerate aristocracy, "only wise because rich, otherwise idiots, illiterate, unfit for any manner of service!" (2.164). A "beggar's child, as *Cardan* well observes, *is no whit inferior to a Prince's, most part better*" (2.168-69).

Such passages, picked from here and there through the *Anatomy*, do not constitute an endorsement of the democratic principle. Burton's quarrel is not with the idea of aristocracy but with the aristocrats. In fact, the social hierarchy which he considers right in principle he finds abominable in reality (see Chap. VII).

III

The tranquil stability which Burton considers the social *summum bonum* would require a reasonable degree of uniformity in religious belief and in forms of worship. Hence it is proper that there should be a single, state-sponsored church to provide and enforce such uniformity. The established church would interpret scripture and exercise at least a loose control over the doctrines preached by its ministers. In conducting worship, it would regularly and universally employ beautiful and impressive rituals. These would manifest the church's present unity and its ties with the past. In theory at least, the Church of England satisfies the requirements. Burton considers England fortunate in having "the Gospel truly preached, Church discipline established" (1.97).

In the lively controversy on the question of ecclesiastical government,[8] Burton stands with the defenders of the existing episcopacy. The church, like the state, is properly governed by a hierarchy deriving its authority from above (and from a temporal source). In his utopia "Ecclesiastical discipline" will be administered by bishops (1.115). He is conscious of abuses in the Church of England; even among the bishops there is corruption (see especially 1.379-80). His utopian scheme provides for

[8] W. H. Frere, in *The English Church in the Reigns of Elizabeth and James I* (London, 1924), reviews the disruptive ecclesiastical disputes of the period during which the *Anatomy* was taking form. See especially pp. 291 ff. See also John R. H. Moorman, *A History of the Church in England* (London, 1953), Chap. XIV; Norman Sykes, *Old Priest and New Presbyter* (Cambridge, 1956), pp. 48-117. Concerning Burton's ideas on the political functions of the church, see Mueller, pp. 81, 83-84.

83

reform in the system of ecclesiastical appointments (1.115). But he never questions the principle of episcopacy.

Burton clearly acknowledges the doctrinal and administrative authority of the episcopal hierarchy (3.484-85). He values, moreover, the traditional ceremonies of the church, which, like the episcopacy, were under vigorous attack in his day. Anthony Wood finds it worthy of record that in his church in the suburbs of Oxford he celebrated the communion with wafers.

He attacks the radical sects which he sees so rapidly gaining strength in England for their rejection of tradition, organization, and authority. These schismatics "will quite demolish all, they will admit of no cere-monies at all . . . no Bishop's-Courts, no Church-government, rail at our Church-discipline . . . no interpretations of Scriptures, no Comments of Fathers, no Councils, but such as their own phantastical spirits dictate, or *recta ratio*, as *Socinians*, by which spirit misled, many times they broach as prodigious paradoxes as" even the Catholics (3.424). The individualistic sectarians threaten the order and regularity of things as they are. Burton advocates suppressive measures which, although they might have seemed mild in the century of the Thirty Years' War, are obviously designed for uncompromising enforcement of conformity (3.433).

Burton is hostile also toward Roman Catholicism. But he exhibits little or none of the individualism which in general has distinguished the various forms of Protestantism. Religion, he believes, properly has a corporate character. The church not only conducts worship according to regular-ized forms but also tells the worshipper what he should believe—conveys to him "the gospel truly preached." "*Brownists, Barrowists, Familists*, and those *Amsterdamian* sects and sectaries, are led all by so many private spirits" (3.425) and are thus damnably misled.

In what he says concerning church polity, Burton seems to assume a uniformity of precept and practice in the Anglican church which did not really exist.

IV

Although Burton is "a philosopher in the broad usage of that word,"[9] he is no metaphysician. He has evidently read metaphysical works by Plato, Aristotle, and Plotinus. He is acquainted with St. Thomas' *Summa* and has at least a little knowledge of the works of Duns Scotus, Ockham, and a few other medieval philosophers. But abstruse speculation has small appeal to his practical mind. He seems irritated with philosophical dispute, with the wranglings of "Scotists, Thomists, Reals, Nominals," Platonists, Aristotelians (3.423; see further in Chap. VII). To him the issues are not important. His metaphysical reading has not greatly influenced his

[9] Llewelyn Powys, "Robert Burton," *Rats in the Sacristy* (London, 1937), p. 185.

thinking. He quotes metaphysical works usually as he quotes the *Aeneid*, for support or embellishment.

But of necessity Burton has a few conventional ideas concerning the nature of things. He attacks impious thinkers who "attribute all to natural causes, that will acknowledge no supreme power" (3.367). There is a beneficent Deity, whose providence, in ways incomprehensible to men, directs human destiny. Among the attributes of God are "Eternity, Omnipotency, Immutability, Wisdom, Majesty, Justice, Mercy, &c., his Beauty is not the least" (3.360). God created the world for the fostering of the human race, which has repaid his bounty with disobedience and perversity. (Although the idea of plural worlds intrigues Burton, it apparently has not affected his fundamental belief that God's creation centers about the race of Adam.) All mundane creatures are subject to man.

The essential man is an immaterial immortal spirit (the highest member of the tripartite soul). "This *reasonable soul*, which *Austin* calls a spiritual substance moving itself, is defined by Philosophers to be *the first substantial act of a natural, human, organical body, by which a man lives, perceives, and understands, freely doing all things, and with election*" (1.188; see also 1.176). Beyond this there is doubt and disagreement concerning the nature and operation of the soul (1.176-77, 185-88). For a time the soul must dwell in the realm of physical phenomena, confined in a physical body. It theoretically has complete control over the body. But because of the corruption of human nature which followed the Original Sin, the soul is sorely troubled, in its efforts toward virtue, by the insubordinate physical nature with which it is allied (1.431, etc.).

Although it has been weakened and corrupted by the Fall, the human will is nevertheless free, and man has moral responsibiilty. God is not the author of sin (1.190). The deterministic doctrines of classical and Arabian philosophers and of modern "Deists" are detestable (1.191, 3.440-43). The stars may incline but not compel (1.235, 3.279-80). Men need not be ruled by biases of personality arising from their physical constitutions.[10]

No secondary cause can necessitate human action, yet God's providence determines the general course of human events. In obscure ways, He inspires—but does not compel—those whom He has chosen as instruments to effect what He has ordained. "*Columbus* did not find out *America* by chance, but God directed him at that time to discover it: it was contingent [not necessitated] to him, but necessary to God; he reveals and conceals, to whom and when he will" (2.69). Our "will is free in respect of us, and things contingent, howsoever (in respect of God's determinate counsel) they are inevitable and necessary" (1.191).

---

[10] Kocher points out Burton's frequent insistence that the melancholiac may help himself if he will make the effort (*Science and Religion*, p. 300). He regards this as evidence of Burton's resistance to the deterministic implications of the physiological psychology on which his psychiatry is based.

Burton does not explain how he reconciles his belief in free will with his predestinarianism (see below) or with his adherence to the Articles of the Church of England, in which one reads that, since the Fall, man "cannot turn and prepare himself, by his own natural strength and good works, to faith, and calling upon God . . ." (Article X). Possibly he subscribes to the Calvinistic opinion that, although Original Sin has deprived man totally of his moral powers, he still has natural talents which, though diminished by Adam's fall, enable him to exercise choice among things morally indifferent (*Institutes*, II, ii).

V

Burton's Christianity is emotional and ethical rather than logical or theological. He does not feel altogether at home among abstractions. He is little interested in God's eternity, omnipotency, and immutability but has a great deal to say about His beauty, His love, and His mercy. He endeavors earnestly to confirm in his reader the faith which is necessary to salvation, and through many pages of his book, gently and movingly urges penitence and obedience to the will of a merciful and loving God.

He seems to find the will of God especially in the Two Commandments. Man should love, forgive, and selflessly aid his neighbor. Yet the love of one's fellow man is of "little worth, if [it] proceed not from a true Christian illuminated soul, if it be not done *in ordine ad Deum*, for God's sake . . . [It is] sustained by Faith and Hope, which with this our Love make . . . an Aequilateral Triangle, *and yet the greatest of them is Love*, I Cor. 13.13" (3.35). This love is humble, long-suffering, self-immolating. For God's sake the Christian "will love his brother, not in word and tongue, but in deed and truth." Mankind would be perfectly happy if all practised Christian charity. "But this we cannot do," and our failure in charity "is the cause of all our woes, miseries, discontent, melancholy . . . We do *invicem angariare*" (3.36-37).

Other Christian virtues which Burton preaches are submission and patience. The compassion which he so abundantly extends to his suffering fellow men shows that Christian charity is natural to him. His satiric indignations indicate that submission and patience are harder for him.

Although he is doubtless well acquainted with the major Christian controversies, Burton gives scanty attention to disputed theological questions. He has little or nothing to say concerning transubstantiation, the Trinity, faith and works, justification, apostolic succession, or resurrection and judgment. He says strangely little about the after life, nothing at all about the joys of Paradise. He makes several horrified references to Arianism, but never explains why it is pernicious. He scornfully attacks certain "superstitious" Roman Catholic beliefs and practices—confession and absolution, the sale of indulgences, the doctrine of Purgatory, opposition to the translation of the Bible, imposition of celibacy upon the clergy, etc.—, but he does not debate the Catholic-Protestant issues. He ridicules the radical Protestant sects of England and deplores their individualism, their prudish condemnation of innocent diversions, and their opposition to church ornament, music, and ceremonial; but he does not demonstrate the errors in their doctrines. He contemns the Socinian religion of reason but does not refute the Socinians. It is hard to believe that he has excluded theological argument from the *Anatomy* because of its remoteness from psychiatry, for he shows no inclination to exclude any other kind of material, even the most remote.

In spite of this relative indifference to doctrinal issues, Burton makes a small contribution to the wordy and angry debate concerning predestination (3.482-85), "the century's most obvious waste of thought."[11] He rejects the Arminian "plausible doctrine of universal grace, which many Fathers, our late *Lutherans* and modern Papists do still maintain, that we have free-will of our selves, and that grace is common to all that will believe." He firmly disapproves certain even "less orthodoxal" beliefs: that the majority of mankind will be saved; that to believe the contrary is to doubt the goodness and omnipotence of God; that pagans who never heard of Christ are saved if they have lived virtuously according to the law of nature; that a just and merciful God would not condemn myriads to the torments of hell for a sin (Adam's) which they did not commit.[12] "But these absurd paradoxes are exploded by our Church, we teach otherwise" (3.482-84).

Election, moreover, did not follow the Fall; God's basis of choice was not foreseen faith (an Arminian tenet) or foreseen works (Roman Catholic); reprobation means explicit condemnation, not merely omission from the body of the elect (it is *"non ex praeteritione"*). "God's absolute decree" was formulated "from the beginning, before the foundation of the world was laid, or *homo conditus*" (3.484). "According to his immutable, eternal, just decree . . . God calls all, and would have all to be saved according to the efficacy of vocation: all are invited, but only the elect apprehended: the rest that are unbelieving, impenitent . . . are in a reprobate sense" (3.485). God's elect are those in whom, in accordance with His unrevealed will, his vocation is efficacious, those who "through Grace obey the calling" (Article XVII).

Burton was one of many early Stuart Anglicans who sought to reconcile the Calvinism incorporated in the Articles of the Church with less rigorous

---

[11] Schultz, *Milton and Forbidden Knowledge*, p. 135.

[12] These opinions Burton has found in *De Amplitudine Beati Regni Dei* (1554), by Celio Secundo Curio. He suggests that the book was written by an impostor. It may be that, because Curio was somewhat eminent among the continental Reformers, Burton is reluctant to believe that he was capable of such heresies. Burton owned a copy of *De Amplitudine*.

doctrines.[13] If a predestinarian clings to belief in individual freedom and responsibility, in the relation between salvation and voluntary merit, in divine mercy extended to all, perhaps even in God's justice, he will find himself involved in logical dilemmas. Indeed one such dilemma is written into the seventeenth of the Articles of the Church: "Predestination to Life is the everlasting purpose of God, whereby (before the foundations of the world were laid) he hath constantly decreed by his counsel secret to us, to deliver from curse and damnation those whom he hath chosen in Christ out of mankind." The term *reprobation* is avoided, but the idea is clearly implied. Toward the end of the article, there is reference to the divine promises "generally set forth to us in Holy Scripture." There "can be no doubt that 'generally' here means 'universally.' "[14] As Burton says, *all* are invited. God's mercy is expressed in this universal invitation. Yet before the foundations of the world were laid, He arbitrarily elected some and rejected others. A god who offers the opportunity of salvation to all without really meaning it is not a merciful or even a candid deity.

There was no easy solution for the logical difficulties encountered by the early Stuart predestinarians who tried to avoid the extreme implications of the doctrine. Possibly there was none better than to acknowledge that there are things which to the human mind seem logically impossible but which are nevertheless possible to God.[15] This, I believe, is Burton's thought, although he never expressly states it.

Whatever his reasoning, Burton is a predestinarian. In comforting those who fear God's rejection, he does not say that God gives every man a second chance or that any man may earn acceptance by voluntary effort to achieve a sounder faith and a more righteous life. The "plausible" Arminian "doctrine of universal grace" is not "orthodoxal." Yet he is not harshly Calvinistic. His emphasis is on grace, not reprobation. No devout man need despair of election: "we must not determine who are [reprobate], condemn ourselves, or others, because we have an universal invitation; all are commanded to believe, and we know not how soon or late before our end we may be received" (3.485). No man who repents and earnestly desires God's approval has been rejected: "no sin at all but

---

[13] See Schultz, pp. 127-40.

[14] Edgar C. S. Gibson, *The Thirty-nine Articles of the Church of England* (London, 1896-97), II, 486. Gibson supports this interpretation by quotation of the *Reformatio Legum Ecclesiasticarum* and I Timothy, 2:4 (pp. 462, 486).

[15] "Freewill and predestination are both taught in the Bible; and though we cannot see at present *how* they are compatible with each other, yet if, in the interests of logical consistency, we are led to deny either one of them, we shall find ourselves involved in errors and difficulties from which there is no escape. For the present we must be content to hold both as *parts* of the truth, remembering that we know but 'in part,' and leaving their complete reconciliation to the time when we 'shall know, even as we are known.' "—Gibson, pp. 479-480.

impenitency can give testimony of final reprobation" (3.481). He reassures the anxious Christian by telling him that his very anxiety proves his election: "A true desire of mercy in the want of mercy, is mercy itself . . . to feel in ourselves the want of grace, and to be grieved for it, is grace itself" (3.475). Although the elect may lapse, their salvation is certain: "we may fall, but not finally" (3.484). Like many of the Puritan ministers of his day,[16] Burton employs the forbidding principle of predestination as a doctrine of reassurance and hope. He is unfaithful neither to the Anglican articles nor to his own compassionate nature.

VI

In his fifth edition (1638) Burton inserts, at the close of the passage on predestination, a suggestion that he has exercised great self-restraint in discussing this subject. He "might have said more" but has refrained because this "is a forbidden question." The "Preface or Declaration to the Articles of the Church, printed 1633, to avoid factions and altercations," prohibits "*all curious search, to print or preach, or draw the Article aside by our own sense and Comments.*" This prohibition is directed at "University Divines especially" (3.485). Burton adds a quotation from Erasmus which advocates submission to tyranny as preferable to sedition.

Although Burton refers to the printing of 1633, the royal declaration in question appeared as preface to the Articles as early as 1628. He must have known of it long before the *Anatomy* of 1632 went to press, yet he says nothing of it in his 1632 edition. His depreciatory reference to the prohibition was evidently prompted by troubles at Oxford in the summer of 1631. These would have occurred too late to affect his revision for the fourth edition but would still have been a sharp memory when he prepared the fifth.[17]

On April 12, 1630, William Laud became chancellor of Oxford. Laud was an Arminian and a rigorous administrator. About a year later, three members of the university challenged authority by preaching sermons of Puritanical character. Abetted by two sympathetic proctors, they evaded the efforts of the vice-chancellor, William Smith, to correct them for what he regarded as defiance of the royal declaration. Smith appealed to the king, possibly at Laud's suggestion and certainly with his support. Charles heard the case on August 23. He expelled the erring ministers from the university and deprived the proctors of their office.[18] This

---

[16] See William Haller, *The Rise of Puritanism* (New York, 1938), pp. 88-91.

[17] Although the fifth edition was not published until 1638, the printing of it began considerably earlier than August of 1635. See Duff, "The Fifth Edition," *Library*, 4th series, IV, 86.

[18] See *The Works of William Laud* (Oxford, 1847-60), III, 214; IV, 49-70; John Rushworth, *Historical Collection* (London, 1659-1701), vol. I, part ii, pp. 110-11; the article on Thomas Ford in the *Dictionary of National Biography*.

89

episode must have been the subject of excited comment and bitter debate throughout Oxford. Apparently the Puritanical ministers had the support of a fairly numerous party.

Being a predestinarian, Burton would naturally sympathize with the insubordinate divines. His remarks on the royal declaration seem to be a timid protest against the suppression of Calvinistic opinion. He must have been deeply disturbed both by Laud's Arminianism and by the severities of his administration. He never mentions Laud, but the chancellor must have been often in his thoughts after 1630, possibly even more often after Laud became archbishop in 1633.

The interpolation concerning the preface to the Articles might suggest that Burton has revised, perhaps severely pruned, his discussion of predestination to conform with the royal injunction. He has not, however, been frightened into retraction. Except for the addition of a half dozen lines concerning Socinianism, the 1638 discourse on predestination is substantially the same as the 1632 version.

This interpolation in the fifth edition is the only evidence in the *Anatomy* of restiveness under authority.

VII

An English minister of the early Stuart period, no matter how much disinclined to disputation, could hardly have avoided taking a stand on three questions which were then agitating the clergy. One of these, a matter of church polity, was the question of episcopacy. Burton was a staunch episcopalian. The second was t' e question of ritual in worship. Burton was a defender of the traditional ceremonies; he is known to have used wafers in conducting the communion. The third was the doctrinal issue of predestination. Burton believed in election and reprobation, finding sanction for his position in the Articles of the Church.

His opinions on church government and on ceremonial worship seem to align him with the Laudian conservatives. Yet doctrinally he stands with the moderate Calvinistic Puritans. His infrequent references to Calvin are all deferential. He attacks many sects with wrath and ridicule, but never the Presbyterians. He has read, apparently with considerable respect, works by various Puritan divines,[19] notably William Perkins, Richard Greenham, and John Downame. These he finds useful especially in his comfort for the despairing conscience. Since he is mildly Calvinistic and Puritanical, his position among early Stuart clergymen is somewhere near the middle point between the extremes.

There is, however, little Puritan acerbity or contentiousness in him. He strongly condemns preachers who terrify their auditors with lurid talk

---

[19] Gottlieb reviews Burton's reading in pious works written in English: *Burton's Knowledge of English Poetry*, pp. 182-228 (Appendix B).

of reprobation (3.456-57). The persistent debate over predestination, he believes, causes much needless misery: "this furious curiosity, needless speculation, fruitless meditation about election, reprobation, free-will, grace, such places of Scripture preposterously conceived, torment still, and crucify the souls of too many, and set all the world together by the ears" (3.482). In his disapproval of quarrelsome disputation, he shares the position of the Anglican rationalists of his day.[20] He deserves an honorable place among the "peacemakers."[21]

VIII

Burton's forebearance does not extend beyond the Lutheran-Calvinist-Anglican area of religious opinion. All other creeds are abominable to him. Though he is relatively indifferent to theological subtleties, he readily recognizes gross impiety. Apparently he has studied the geographical distribution of religions and has made some appalling discoveries. Christendom constitutes only a fraction of the world. Most worshippers in this fraction are *"Pseudo-Christians"* (3.417), believers in false doctrines. There are, moreover, many men of no faith at all and many professing Christians whose piety is so faint and whose way of life is so un-Christian that they also might be considered infidels.

Burton fervidly denounces the major religions which have led men astray (3.397 ff.). He writes scathing comments on several pagan forms of worship, particularly the ancient Greek religion (the gods of the ancient world were masquerading devils) and modern Mohammedanism. His most caustic language, however, is directed at the Roman Catholic Church, which for centuries held all western Europe in spiritual bondage. The effects of Roman Catholic "superstition" among men have been prodigious and calamitous. His attacks on Catholicism recur through the *Anatomy*.

The Reformation, by its eradication of the deep-rooted errors of Catholicism, seemed to promise purification of Christianity. Luther came and "as another Sun" began "to drive away those foggy mists of superstition, to restore . . . that purity of the Primitive Church. And after him many good and godly men, divine spirits, have done their endeavours, and still do" (3.423). But the Devil is pertinacious and indefatigable. Among Protestants there have appeared corrupters of doctrine on the left instead of the right, "a mad giddy company of Precisians, Schismaticks, and some Hereticks, even in our bosoms in another extreme . . . that out of too much zeal in opposition to [Catholicism] . . . will quite demolish all." The Protestant extremists reject all forms of church discipline, all ritual and

[20] See Haller, pp. 242-48.
[21] Schultz, pp. 157-83.

music, and all doctrine "but such as their own phantastical spirits dictate" (3.424). Christian truth does not yet prevail.

Burton assails not only those who believe erroneously but also those deficient in faith or virtue: "impious Epicures, Libertines, Atheists, Hypocrites, Infidels, worldly, secure, impenitent, unthankful, and carnal-minded men, that attribute all to natural causes, that will acknowledge no supreme power; that have cauterized consciences, or live in a reprobate sense" (3.367). Toward this miscellaneous company of sinners he directs much hot invective. More than any others, he loathes and contemns "*Herodian* temporizing States-men, politick Machiavelians and Hypocrites, that make a show of Religion" for their selfish ends "but in their hearts laugh at it" (3.446).

Toward philosophical sceptics, however, he is a little milder, for their incredulity arises from intellectual difficulties, not from mere desire for freedom in self-indulgence. He reviews several heretical philosophical opinions: the idea that the multiplicity of diverse religions indicates that all are in error; the belief that the suffering of the virtuous precludes the existence of a beneficent God; the attribution of "all to natural causes" (the opinion of "a Philosopher, a *Galenist*, an *Averroist,* [or] with *Rabelais* a Physician, a Peripatetick, an Epicure," 3.440); the doctrine (from Seneca) that God is "so tied to second causes, to that inexorable necessity, that he could alter nothing of that which was once decreed." "Thus perverse men cavil" (3.443), says Burton, but he does not confute them.

On the question of religious toleration, Burton takes what he believes to be the middle ground. Some, he says, advocate "a general toleration," complete freedom of worship. He cannot subscribe to anything so extreme. "The *medium* is best, and that which *Paul* prescribes, *Gal.* 6.1." One should attempt to correct the erring brother with "*gentle admonitions*"; if these fail, "he must be excommunicate . . . delivered over to Satan. *Immedicabile vulnus ense recidendum est.* . . . For the vulgar, restrain them by laws, mulcts, burn their books, forbid their conventicles: for when the cause is taken away, the effect will soon cease. Now for Prophets, dreamers, and such rude silly fellows," medical treatment is appropriate (3.433). In a century when "club law, fire and sword" (3.432-33) were the usual means of dealing with heretics, Burton's proposals were moderate.

Yet he shows rather an inclination towards mildness in enforcing conformity than a genuine spirit of tolerance. When he writes on religion, Burton is not his usual reasonable and temperate self. He gives no fair hearing to those who differ with him, and his confutation tends to be merely angry invective. Sometimes, however, his sanity overcomes the stubbornness of his convictions: "Our Papists object . . . to us, and account us hereticks, we them; the *Turks* esteem of both as Infidels, and we them as a company of Pagans, Jews against all; when indeed there is a general fault in us all, and something in the very best, which may justly deserve God's wrath" (3.428). The un-Christian strife among Christians grieves him deeply.

IX

A distinctive feature of Burton's treatment of religious themes is his continual employment of his psychological learning and insight. The combination of the parson's and psychiatrist's views is suggested by the title of the last section of the *Anatomy*: "Religious Melancholy." This concerns all heresies, impieties, and diffidences.

The author gives good reason for connecting men's infidelities with their melancholy. The melancholy humor "is *balneum diaboli*, as *Serapio* holds, the Devil's bath, and invites him to come to it" (3.478; *cf.* 1.493). Melancholy makes men irrational and suggestible and thus renders them easy and tempting victims of the diabolic malice. The Devil, then, is the efficient cause of religious melancholy.[22]

Because he has no precedent for setting up religious melancholy as a separate category, Burton is a little hesitant and apologetic: "I have no pattern to follow . . . No Physician hath as yet distinctly written of it" (3.358). As a matter of fact, Burton has found in his medical authorities a good many accounts of the melancholies of the over-pious, and various English ministers of his own period are concerned over the distinction between the morbid melancholy sense of sin and the true affliction of conscience.[23] Yet his treatise on religious melancholy, as he suggests, was something essentially new.

The term *religious melancholy* is not really sharply defined in Burton's mind. He uses it sometimes literally, sometimes semi-metaphorically. Literally the term means mental aberration in which black bile is involved and which manifests itself in some kind of irrational religious deviation. Semi-metaphorically it embraces all religious error and disbelief. Since melancholy is "a disease of the soul" and since it takes multifarious forms, this comprehensive extension of meaning is not altogether figurative. In the following I shall confine myself to religious error connected literally with black bile.

Often both cause and effect are of a religious character. The inordinately pious are highly susceptible. Self-mortification, solitude, and long con-

[22] Kocher traces the progress toward rationalism and naturalism of Renaissance ideas concerning Satan's supposed powers and activities (*Science and Religion*, pp. 119-45). For his period, Burton's beliefs about these matters were not advanced.
[23] See *Elizabethan Malady*, pp. 47-54. The basic purpose of Bright's *Treatise of Melancholie* is the drawing of this distinction. See the prefatory note "To His Melancholicke friend: M."

93

tinued meditation on questions of faith and salvation engender the melancholy humor, and this in turn affects the phantasy and misleads the intellectual faculty. Immoderate "fasting, bad diet, sickness, melancholy, solitariness" give the Devil his "best opportunity . . . to delude them" (3.393). Men become "quite mortified and mad" through their efforts to win merit "by penance, going woolward, whipping, alms, fasting, &c. An. 1320, there was a Sect of whippers in *Germany*, that . . . lashed, and cruelly tortured themselves" (3.392). Of melancholy persons possessed by the Devil "stupend things are said . . . their actions, gestures, *contortions,* fasting, prophesying, speaking languages they were never taught, &c." (1.164). The *Anatomy* includes an astonishing collection of tales concerning demonic possession (1.228-30).

Burton distinguishes two principal kinds of religious melancholy, that of *excess* and that of *defect*. His terms suggest once more his distrust of extremes.

Error and fanaticism are the symptoms which distinguish religious melancholy in excess. No man can love God too much, but there are many who "are zealous without knowledge, and too solicitous about that which is not necessary" (3.366). The patients include all those who proclaim novel heresies and all who believe themselves divinely favored with spiritual powers. "*Some seem to be inspired of the Holy Ghost, some take upon them to be Prophets, some are addicted to new opinions, some foretell strange things, de statu mundi et Antichristi, saith Gordonius. Some will prophesy of the end of the World to a day almost, and the fall of the Antichrist, . . . as Laurentius holds*" (3.358). The "enthusiasts" and "schismatics" who lead the extreme Protestant sects are melancholy men deluded by the Devil.

Religious melancholy in defect refers to weakness of faith or to outright disbelief. The form of it which interests Burton most is an excruciating diffidence. Patients develop a morbid consciousness of their wickedness and, forgetting the all-embracing love and mercy of God, despair of salvation. There are of course men whose affliction of conscience is rationally grounded, whose sins actually warrant a fear of damnation. Burton is concerned, however, only with those whose despair is due to melancholy. In these, the melancholy humor, often due to excessive fasting and solitary meditation on religious questions, engenders pathological fears. "Fear takes away their content, and dries the blood, wasteth the marrow, alters their countenance" (3.463).[24] "The heart is grieved, the conscience wounded, and the mind eclipsed with black fumes arising from those perpetual terrors" (3.452). Fear engenders melancholy and melan-

[24] Fear and sorrow are "cold and dry" passions. They deprive the blood of its vital heat and moisture and thus cause it to degenerate into melancholy. See *Elizabethan Malady*, pp. 12-15.

choly engenders fear in a vicious cycle. The patient develops the melancholy delusion that his transgressions are beyond forgiveness.

Many are terrified by imaginary demons and hellfire. Because they suppose themselves the objects of "God's heavy wrath, a most intolerable pain and grief of heart seizeth on them; to their thinking they are already damned, they suffer the pains of Hell . . . they smell brimstone, talk familiarly with Devils, hear and see *Chimeras*, prodigious, uncouth shapes . . . they roar and howl, curse, blaspheme, deny God . . . and are still ready to offer violence unto themselves" (3.485). A person in this condition is not to be blamed for his "blasphemous, impious, unclean thoughts." These "proceed not from him, but from a crazed phantasy, distempered humours, black fumes which offend his brain." They are "the Devil's sins" (3.478).

The religious melancholic may alternate between the extremes. If he does so, he will sometimes be "inspired by the Holy Ghost, full of the spirit: one while he is saved, another while damned, or still troubled in mind for his sins, the Devil will surely have him, &c." (1.465).

The treatment for religious melancholy may be both physical and mental. As for "Prophets, dreamers, and such rude silly fellows, that through fasting, too much meditation, preciseness, or by Melancholy are distempered: the best means to reduce them *ad sanam mentem* is to alter their course of life, and with conference, threats, promises, persuasions, to intermix Physick" (3.433). For despairing patients also medical treatment is proper. Physic is "God's instrument, and not unfit. The Devil works by mediation of humours, and mixt diseases must have mixt remedies" (3.490). The physical therapy for either kind of religious melancholy is the same as that suitable for other melancholies: "diet, air, exercise. . . . They must not be left solitary . . . never idle." Counsel, comfort, and the applying of "God's Word to their distressed souls" are perhaps even more effective. Burton lists several authors of "excellent Exhortations . . . to this purpose" (3.468) and then writes one of his own, the long consolatory discourse with which the *Anatomy* closes.

Burton's discourse of black melancholy fumes and of the Devil's machinations is more interesting than convincing to us of the twentieth century. Yet we should give him credit for perceiving, as few did in his period, that fanaticism and despair are related to mental abnormality. We should notice also that the religious intolerance of Burton the parson is considerably qualified by the understanding and sympathy of Burton the psychiatrist.

Chapter VII: MAN'S UNREASON

LIKE MANY OTHER Renaissance treatises on psychology, the *Anatomy* proper begins with a panegyric on human nature. Man is "the most excellent and noble" of God's earthly creatures, the audacious miracle of Nature, "*the Abridgement and Epitome of the World . . . Microcosmos,* a little world, Sovereign Lord of the Earth . . . *Imaginis Imago,* created to God's own *Image*" (1.149). He is endowed with a reasonable, immortal soul and with all faculties and capabilities which he needs to achieve happiness in this life and salvation hereafter.

But man is superlatively wretched. This is due ultimately to the sin of Adam, instigated by the Devil, from which proceeded "that general corruption of mankind . . . all bad inclinations, and actual transgressions, which cause our several calamities" (1.150). Man "was at first pure, divine, perfect, happy . . . put in Paradise, to know God, to praise and glorify him, to do his will" (1.149). In his degenerate state, however, he is "a castaway, a caitiff, one of the most miserable creatures of the world . . . so much obscured by his fall (that some few reliques excepted) he is inferior to a beast" (1.149-50). Since only a few relics of the light of reason remain to man, he can achieve virtue and happiness only through great and unremitting effort.

Human misery is God's punishment for sin, Adam's and our own (1.150-55). God sometimes employs nature as His instrument, chastising men by plagues, earthquakes, floods, the depredations of wild beasts, etc. (1.153-54). The principal evidence of the divine wrath, however, is the weakness of man's psychological and moral powers, sadly enfeebled by the Fall. The consequence of this weakness is that, through unreasonableness and feebleness of will, we torment one another and ourselves. It is our own folly "which crucifies us most." By yielding to our passions, we sacrifice our human nature, degenerate into bestiality, and provoke an angry God to "heap upon us this [affliction] of *Melancholy,* and all kinds of incurable diseases, as a just and deserved punishment of our sins" (1.156).

Reason dictates obedience to the will of God, particularly the practice of the Christian virtue of charity. But human conduct is seldom motivated by love: the cause of all our woes is "want of this charity. We do *invicem angariare,* insult, contemn, vex, torture, molest, and hold one another's noses to the grind-stone hard. . . . Monsters of men as we are," we fight and snarl like beasts over the world's prizes. We "break one another's backs, and both are ruined and consumed in the end." We do not care "how many thousands we undo." Our wealth may be fabulous, but we will not share it. Although "our poor brother" be "in great extremity," we "spend it idly, consume it with dogs, hawks, hounds, unnecessary buildings, in riotous apparel, ingurgitate, or let it be lost," rather than relieve him (3.37-38). But we win no happiness through our irrational behavior; we succeed only in enhancing our own misery.

II

Warfare exhibits the tragic consequences of man's irrational selfishness on a large scale.[1] War is the most savage and destructive of the calamities which man inflicts upon man. There are "so many bloody battles, so many thousand slain at once, such streams of blood able to turn mills . . . to make sport for princes, without any just cause, *for vain trifles* . . . whilst statesmen . . . are secure at home, pampered with all delights & pleasures." The soldiers who suffer for such trivial reasons are fine specimens of manhood. They are "led like so many beasts to the slaughter, in the flower of their years, pride, and full strength . . . killed up as so many sheep for devil's food, 40,000 at once. At once, said I?—that were tolerable, but these wars last always" (1.58-59).

Characteristically Burton does not renounce war absolutely: not all wars are "to be condemned, as those fantastical *Anabaptists* vainly conceive. Our Christian Tacticks are all out as necessary as the *Roman Acies*, or *Grecian* Phalanx" (1.62). It is necessary that the Christian commonwealth be prepared to protect itself and that it fight on occasion. In his utopia Burton provides "forces still ready at a small warning, by land and sea," to defend the state (1.122). But he condemns "Offensive wars, except the cause be very just." When such wars must be waged, soldiers should "abstain as much as is possible from depopulations, burning of towns, massacring of infants, &c." (1.121-22).

To "be a soldier is a most noble and honourable profession (as the world is) not to be spared, they are our best walls and bulwarks" (1.62). In the social scheme of the utopia, soldiers occupy the second rank of relative dignity, scholars the first (1.116). Valor "is much to be commended in a wise man." But men are unable to distinguish true valor. They mistake "theft, murder, and rapine . . . rapes, slaughters, massacres, &c." for honorable action (1.63). Murderers and ravagers are universally admired, "have statues, crowns, pyramids, obelisks, to their eternal fame" (1.60).

War is inhuman and un-Christian: "Who made so soft and peaceable a creature, born to love, mercy, meekness" to engage in this brutish mutual destruction? "How may Nature expostulate with mankind, *Ego te divinum*

---

[1] Burton's ideas concerning war are much like those of Erasmus. See Robert P. Adams, "The Literary Thought on War and Peace in English Literature of the Renaissance," *American Philosophical Society: Year Book 1955*, pp. 272-77, and "Erasmus' Ideas of His Role as a Social Critic ca. 1480-1500," *Renaissance News*, XI (1958), 11-16.

97

animal finxi, &c.! I made thee a harmless, quiet, a divine creature! How may God expostulate, and all good men!" (1.60). Burton is appalled especially by wars fought in the name of Christ.

III

As he looks at man in his social relations, Burton sees much that is unreasonable and unjust.[2]

The social hierarchy which he considers right in principle, he finds abominable in reality. For those who by hereditary privilege rule the commonwealth abuse their powers grossly. He sees that so it is in England, and his reading in history and biography reveals to him that thus it has always been. "Princes and Potentates are immoderate in lust [*cf.* 3.68], hypocrites, epicures, of no religion, but in show [*cf.* 3.377-80] . . . malicious, envious, factious, ambitious, emulators, they tear a common-wealth asunder" (1.90). They are unlettered and stupid, "wise only by inheritance, and in authority by birth-right, favour, or for their wealth and titles . . . such men are not always fit . . . it must needs turn to the confusion of a State" (1.91).

As for the English gentry, Burton sees them as complacent, ignorant, and slothful: "amongst us the Badge of Gentry is idleness, to be . . . a drone, *fruges consumere natus,* to have no necessary employment . . . in Church and Commonwealth" (2.81. See also 1.278, 280-81). He deplores the inordinate and frivolous extravagance of the highly born (1.123-24, 2.106). The "ancient characters of true Gentry" are exemplified in the man who is "more affable, courteous, gently disposed, of fairer carriage, better temper, of a more magnanimous, heroical, and generous spirit, than . . . ordinary boors and peasants" (2.165). Burton has seen little enough of these qualities in the gentry. Most gentlemen have a very different conception of gentility: if a man "*can hawk and hunt, ride an horse, play at cards and dice, swagger, drink, swear,* take tobacco with a grace, sing, dance, wear his clothes in fashion . . . insult, scorn, strut, contemn others, and use a little mimical and apish compliment above the rest, he is a complete (*Egregiam vero laudem!*) a well-qualified gentleman" (2.160). Because of the character and deportment of the ruling classes, there is misrule, injustice, and tribulation in England.

Another major social evil (a related phenomenon) is the great concentration of wealth in unworthy hands. The rich indulge in frivolous and ruinously expensive pleasures—"Cards, Dice, Hawks, & Hounds"—and spend prodigally on "mad phantastical buildings . . . Galleries, Cloisters, Terraces, Walks, Orchards, Gardens, Pools, Rillets, Bowers" (1.333).

[2] Burton's views on various social evils are discussed, more or less fully, in Evans, *Psychiatry of Robert Burton,* pp. 91-97; Patrick, "Robert Burton's Utopianism," pp. 354-58; Mueller, *Anatomy of Robert Burton's England,* pp. 52-62.

They dress ostentatiously, absurdly, and wastefully; in appearance they are a "company of counterfeit vizards, whifflers, *Cuman* asses, maskers, mummers, painted puppets, outsides, phantastick shadows, gulls, monsters, giddy-heads, butterflies" (1.54). They have "a natural contempt of learning" and an "innate idleness"; "great wealth & little wit go commonly together" (1.131). They are wholly irresponsible. By their heartless frivolity and greed, they multiply the miseries of the poor. They do not hesitate, for example, to drive farmers from their fields (they *"fling down country Farms, and whole Towns"*) in order to create game preserves (1.334) or to provide pasturage for profitable sheep ("sheep demolish towns, devour men," 1.73). While the wealthy man "feasts, revels . . . hath variety of robes, sweet musick, ease, . . . many an hunger-starved poor creature pines in the street, wants clothes to cover him, labours hard all day long" (1.320).

Riches do not bring happiness. A certain man "is rich, wealthy, fat; what gets he by it? pride, insolency, lust, ambition, cares, fears, suspicion, trouble, anger, emulation, and many filthy diseases of body and mind . . . [The wealthy] are like painted walls, fair without, rotten within: diseased, filthy, crazy, full of intemperate effects." Anyone who knew the anxieties which they suffer would *"renounce all riches"* (2.169). The corollary is that poverty fosters virtue, health, and contentment (2.167-199). But Burton is not really convinced by his own moralizing. He has a keen consciousness of the miseries of poverty and sees clearly that indigence and moral rectitude are not actually concomitant (1.403-11). For himself, he would choose neither wealth nor poverty but a moderate competency (1.14, 412).

On all levels of society he sees insolent pride coupled with an ignoble servility which is motivated by ambition and avarice. Everywhere men are "an inconsiderate multitude" of sycophants; "like so many dogs in a village, if one bark, all bark without a cause: as fortune's fan turns, if a man be in favour, or commended by some great one, all the world applauds him; if in disgrace, in an instant all hate him" (1.71). A person of wealth and rank, no matter how undeserving and base he may be, is courted and fawned upon: "God bless his good Worship! his Honour! every man speaks well of him . . . sues to him for his love, favour, & protection, to serve him, belong unto him . . . though he be an auf, a ninny, a monster, a goosecap . . . What cookery, masking, mirth, to exhilarate his person! . . . What sport will your Honour have? hawking, hunting, fishing, fowling, bulls, bears, cards, dice, cocks, players, tumblers, fiddlers, jesters, &c., they are at your good Worship's command" (1.400-01). The rich man himself "loathes and scorns his inferior, hates or emulates his equal, envies his superior, insults over all such as are under him, as if he were of another *species*, a demi-god" (1.320).

Although he sees the reasonableness of desire for moderate wealth, Burton is shocked by the greed of human kind and the enormities which it moves men to commit. The desire for gold "will make a man run to the *Antipodes*, or tarry at home and turn parasite, lie, flatter, prostitute himself, swear and bear false witness; he will venture his body, kill a king, murder his father, and damn his soul to come at it" (3.20).

Avarice makes men fiercely quarrelsome. They engage continually in litigation: "for every toy and trifle they go to law . . . they are ready to pull out one another's throats; and for commodity *to squeeze blood,* saith *Hierome, out of their brother's heart,* defame, lie . . . spend their goods, lives, fortunes, friends, undo one another, to enrich an *Harpy* Advocate, that preys upon them both, and cries *eia, Socrates! eia, Xanthippe!* or some corrupt Judge" (1.68).

Although he honors "all good laws, and worthy lawyers," Burton considers lawyers in general "a purse-milking nation, a clamorous company, gowned vultures" (1.92) and expatiates upon their higgling perversions of justice. "*Plato* made it a great sign of an intemperate and corrupt Commonwealth, where Lawyers and Physicians did abound" (2.240). In fact the law and its administrators provide no justice. Burton sees "so many lawyers, advocates, so many tribunals, so little justice; so many magistrates, so little care of the common good; so many laws, yet never more disorders" (1.66). In planning his utopia, he gives a good deal of attention to laws and the legal system (1.114-16).

Since men universally disregard reason and follow the promptings of selfish passions, they are everywhere misgoverned. The honest and competent are not permitted to rule. The world's "dignities, honours, offices, are not always given by desert or worth, but for love, affinity, friendship, affection, great men's letters, or, as commonly, they are bought and sold" (2.218). A fool may hold high office and be respected as "learned, grave, and wise," while "he that is most worthy wants employment, he that hath skill to be a Pilot wants a Ship, and he that could govern a Commonwealth, a world itself, a King in conceit, wants means to exercise his worth, hath not a poor office to manage" (2.219). An ignorant, "base impudent ass" can push ahead "because he can put himself forward, because he looks big . . . or hath good store of friends and money, whereas a more discreet, modest, and better deserving, man shall lie hid, or have a repulse. 'Twas so of old, and ever will be" (2.220).

How are the reasonable, temperate, and righteous to succeed in the world? Burton attempts to console the poor and obscure man: "Let them go on, get wealth, offices, titles . . . by chance, fraud . . . by bribery, flattery, and parasitical insinuation, by impudence, and time-serving, let them climb up to advancement in despite of virtue" (2.216). But he himself is not consoled.

IV

Among the poor and neglected are two overlapping classes to both of which Burton belongs: the university scholars and the minor Anglican clergy. "Poverty is the *Muse's* Patrimony" (1.358). In ancient times intelligent and beneficent kings and nobles supported and rewarded scholarship and the arts (1.367-68), but in Jacobean England the intellectual class is at the mercy of vain and ignorant patrons whose despotic power is due to accidents of birth and fortune. The injustice and indignity of this situation rankle deeply: "To see a scholar crouch and creep to an illiterate peasant for a meal's meat; a scrivener better paid for an obligation; a falconer receive greater wages than a student: a lawyer get more in a day than a philosopher in a year, better reward for an hour than a scholar for a twelvemonth's study; him that can paint *Thais*, play on a fiddle, curl hair, &c., sooner get preferment than a philologer or a poet!" (1.72).

The scholar undergoes a long and grinding course of study at the university to gain his degree. In his devotion to the all-absorbing task of acquiring learning, he sacrifices much: health, wealth, the pleasures of normal social living, sometimes even his sanity. He cuts a sorry figure. Scholars "are most part lean, dry, ill coloured. . . . How many poor scholars have lost their wits, or become dizzards . . . accounted ridiculous and silly fools, idiots, asses." Even "if they keep their wits, yet they are esteemed scrubs and fools by reason of their carriage." Because they lack the social graces, they are derided "by our gallants. Yea, many times, such is their misery, they deserve it: a mere scholar, a mere ass." Scholars are so incapable in practical affairs that even those who "can measure the heavens, range over the world," can be "circumvented by every base tradesman" (1.351-53).

For all his great sacrifices, there is no bright future for the scholar. "*Mercury* can help [him] to knowledge, but not to money" (1.350). What are a scholar's opportunities? He may "teach a School, turn Lecturer or Curate, and for that he shall have Falconer's wages . . . so long as he can please his Patron or the Parish" (1.355). It is no wonder that scholars are "servile and poor," that they "complain pitifully . . . to their respectless Patrons" (1.357). Sycophants who are willing to humor the gentry, even in matters of faith, hold the church livings, and meanwhile "we that are University men . . . wither away as a flower ungathered in a garden, & are never used: or, as too many candles, illuminate ourselves alone" (1.373).

If after a long wait and much effort, a university man obtains a small benefice, he immediately finds himself involved in financial and other practical difficulties so vexing that he becomes "weary of his place, if not his life" (1.374). Because of his patron's stinginess, he may have to labor part-time at a humble trade to make ends meet (1.36). His only company will be rustics and small-town tradesmen; he is "now banished from the Academy, all commerce of the Muses, and confined to a country village, as *Ovid* was from *Rome* to *Pontus*," and must "daily converse with a company of idiots and clowns" (1.374). He is, moreover, wholly at the mercy of a stupid and indifferent patron. "Like an ass, he wears out his time for provender . . . an old torn gown, an ensign of his infelicity, he hath his labour for his pain, a *modicum* to keep him till he be decrepit, and that is all . . . if he offend his good Patron, or displease his Lady Mistress . . . he shall be dragged forth of doors by the heels, away with him!" (1.355-56).

Burton is a firm believer in the social utility of reason, learning, and wisdom. From no other class of its citizens might the commonwealth gain more than from its learned men. But the scholar's acquirements are not valued; no man has less chance than he of rising to a post of high responsibility. Burton himself employs his scholarship, which might be of great practical value to the state, in hatching a vain empire, his utopia.

The scholar's exclusion from the rewards and responsibilities of the world is due to the world's stupid unperceptiveness and indifference. Both university and church, however, harbor evils which are within their own power of correction. These are possibly the most disturbing of all the social abuses which Burton sees, for the university and the church are the two social institutions in which, if in any, one should find the rule of reason and justice.

In the university Burton sees blockheads granted degrees by venal authorities merely because they have the money to pay the fees. "Philosophasters who have no art become Masters of Arts: and the authorities bid those be wise who are endowed with no wisdom, and bring nothing to their degree but the desire to take it. Theologasters, sufficiently and more than sufficiently learned if they but pay the fees, emerge full-blown B. D.'s and D. D.'s" (1.378).[3]

In the church, the "dolts, clods, asses" whom the universities have graduated shove away the worthy bidden guest. They "burst with unwashed feet into the sacred precincts of Theology, bringing nothing but a brazen countenance, some vulgar trash, and scholastic trifles." These vagabonds "basely prostitute our Divinity; these are they who fill pulpits, creep into noblemen's houses." Since they are fitted for no other respectable employment, they "flee to this sacred refuge, clutching at the Priesthood by hook or by crook, not in sincerity, but, as Paul says, 'making merchandise of the word of God.' . . . sacred Theology is polluted by these idiots and mountebanks, and the heavenly Muses prostituted as some common thing." Not even the bishops are guiltless. "For ofttimes the very

[3] This is Shilleto's translation of Burton's Latin.

highest men are perverted by avarice, and . . . lead the way to Simony."
They live luxuriously and indulge in "Sybaritic drinking-parties," while
men of learning and merit "languish in obscurity" (1.378-80).[4]

Burton's *Philosophaster*, written in 1606 and performed February 16,
1617/18 (1.375), shows that he became acutely aware of academic and
ecclesiastical evils many years before the publication of the *Anatomy*. In
his comedy, as in his treatise, he expresses his contempt for pedantic
jargon, for learned pretense, and for the venality of clerical ignoramuses.
The play is sunnier, less mordant, and less effective than the pertinent
passages in the *Anatomy*, but in both works there is vigorous satiric protest against the absurdity, greed, and imposture of the philosophasters
who have corrupted the academic world.

V

Scholars, even when they are learned, are not always wise; churchmen,
even when they are sincerely devoted to religion, are not always right-
thinkers. Both lay scholarship and theology tend to become "vain philosophy" or "curiosity."[5]

Burton is proud of his membership in the community of the learned,
yet he perceives and deplores its intellectual sins. He sees much expense of
intellectual energy in the recording of trivia, in malicious controversy,
and in seeking the answers to questions of no consequence. Scholars search
out "all the ruins of wit, *ineptiarum delicias*, amongst the rubbish of old
writers; *pro stultis habent nisi aliquid sufficiant invenire, quod in aliorum
scriptis vertant vitio*, all fools with them that cannot find fault." They
"puzzle themselves to find out how many streets in *Rome*, houses, gates,
towers, *Homer's* country, *Aeneas'* mother, *Niobe's* daughters, *an Sappho
publica fuerit? ovum prius exstiterit an gallina? &c.*" When they have
made their petty discoveries, they are "as proud, as triumphant . . . as if
they had won a City, or conquered a Province." They "prefer a manuscript many times before the Gospel itself" and make themselves ridiculous
"with their *deleaturs, alii legunt sic, meus codex sic habet*, with their
postremae editiones, annotations, castigations, &c." If their conclusions are
questioned, "they are mad, up in arms on a sudden" (1.129). No strife is
so vainglorious or so bitter as the "tempest of contention" among pedants
(1.34).

Even theology, "the Queen of the professions," has been rendered
absurd and vicious by men's perversity and pride. Too often it is devoted
to frivolous questions and distinctions and sometimes attempts to push
beyond the limitations divinely imposed upon human knowledge. Burton

---

[4] Shilleto's translation. Mueller, pp. 85-88, discusses Burton's attacks on abuses in
the church.
[5] See Chap. V, note 23, and *Anatomy* 1.420-21.

finds these tendencies especially among medieval (Roman Catholic) thinkers. These men "have coined a thousand idle questions, nice distinctions, subtilties, Obs and Sols, such tropological, allegorical expositions, to salve all appearances, objections, such quirks and quiddities, *Quodlibetaries* . . ." They have proposed "a rabble of idle controversies and questions, *an Papa sit Deus, an quasi Deus? An participet utramque Christi naturam?* Whether it be as possible for God to be an Humble-Bee, or a Gourd, as a man? Whether he can . . . make a Whore a Virgin? . . . Whether God can make another God like unto himself?" (3.423). Some "paint [God] in the habit of an old man, and make Maps of Heaven, number the Angels, tell their several names, offices. . . . Why doth [God] suffer so much mischief and evil to be done, if he be able to help? why doth he not assist good, or resist bad, reform our wills, if he be not the author of sin . . . ?" Theologians raise many other "absurd and brainsick questions . . . excrements of curiosity, &c. which, as our Saviour told his inquisitive Disciples, are not fit for them to know" (2.68-69).

The behavior of the learned is often very far from the intellectual humility proper to man. Man should be content to wait in patience for such revelations as God may choose to make: "when God sees his time, he will reveal these mysteries" (2.69). Though the reasons for His dispensation are not always clear, we must not presume to examine them: "he hath reasons reserved to himself, which our frailty cannot apprehend" (3.486).

VI

The surest guide and greatest comfort available to men in the midst of their earthly tribulations is—or should be—religion. But men have, through their wrong-headedness, curiosity, pride, greed, and self-indulgence, distorted and corrupted the basic principles of religion until most religious truth is error and most worship heresy or idolatry (see Chap. VI, sec. viii). Thus men augment their own temporal misery and, what is worse, jeopardize their immortal souls. Religious melancholy (which here means false belief) "more besots and infatuates men" than any other. It does "more harm . . . hath more crucified the souls of mortal men (such hath been the Devil's craft) than wars, plagues, sicknesses, dearth, famine, and all the rest" (3.359). In one way or another, religion produces more misery, here and hereafter, than any other cause.

Christianity, since it has drifted far from its primitive purity, has contributed more than its share. "That the Devil is most busy amongst us that are of the true Church, appears by" the numerous heresies which have arisen among Christians (3.417). Self-seeking or wrong-thinking teachers have led multitudes of the untutored and undiscriminating to place "*novelties and toys*" before the essentials of religion and "*falsehood before truth*" (3.418). As a result many millions suffer agony because they believe that the false or trivial is consequential, in their ignorance neglecting that which is truly essential to salvation.

Teachers and leaders of most Christian denominations have impoverished the lives and tormented the consciences of their followers by condemnation of innocent and natural pleasures: in all "superstitious edicts, we crucify one another without a cause, barring ourselves of many good and lawful things, honest disports, pleasures and recreations . . . Feasts, mirth, musick, hawking, hunting, singing, dancing, &c." God has given us these "to refresh, ease, solace and comfort us. But we are some of us too stern, too rigid, too precise" (3.429; *cf.* 3.424, 457). Rightly understood, Christianity is not a harshly ascetic religion.

The Roman Catholic Church has caused incalculable wretchedness. It has introduced many absurd beliefs and practices: "Purgatory . . . Mass, adoration of Saints . . . Images, Shrines, musty Reliques, Excommunications, confessions, satisfactions, blind obediences, vows, pilgrimages" (3.420). The church prefers "Traditions before Scriptures" and its own ordinances before God's precepts and commandments. The common people are kept so ignorant and subservient by "strict discipline, and servile education, that upon pain of damnation they dare not break the least ceremony, tradition, edict: hold it a greater sin to eat a bit of meat in Lent than kill a man" (3.421).

Burton somewhat shrilly accuses Popes and prelates of distorting Christianity and of misleading the multitudes to fill their purses and gratify their pride. While "the ruder sort" are "gulled and tortured by their superstitions, their own too credulous simplicity and ignorance, their *Epicurean* Popes and *Hypocritical* Cardinals laugh in their sleeves" and enjoy their luxuries and pleasures (3.422). The Pope, indeed, is Antichrist.

Protestant churchmen of the more moderate sects also cause much needless misery. Burton has heard "thundering Ministers" (3.456), preaching apparently from Anglican pulpits, who "are wholly for judgment . . . there is no mercy with them, no salvation, no balsam for their [parishioners'] diseased souls, they can speak of nothing but reprobation, hellfire, and damnation." They "pronounce them damned in all auditories . . . making every small fault and thing indifferent an irremissible offence [and thus] rent, tear, and wound men's consciences." The Catholics "terrify men's souls with purgatory. . . . Our indiscreet Pastors many of them come not far behind" in their preaching "of election, predestination, reprobation *ab aeterno*" (3.457). The pastors who preach thus offend through failure in wisdom; they are not, like the Catholic prelates, self-seeking hypocrites.

The left wing Protestant leaders do much harm with their misdirected enthusiasm. These zealots are "Great Precisians of mean conditions and very illiterate." Because of "a preposterous zeal, fasting, meditation, melancholy," they fall into "gross errors and inconveniences." Burton's scorn for the sectarian leaders is tempered with pity, for they are not deliberate deceivers. They are deluded, mentally ill; they have "more need of Hellebore than those that are in Bedlam" (3.426). Yet their preaching is perniciously effective among the poor and ignorant. "What are all our *Anabaptists, Brownists, Barrowists, Familists,* but a company of rude, illiterate, capricious base fellows?" (3.390).

Thus, as he reviews the history and present state of Christianity, Burton sees that there have always been and will always be false leaders "to dementate men's minds, to seduce and captivate their souls" (3.418). The true religion is so distorted that it brings men, not truth and solace, but wretchedness in this life and damnation hereafter.

Christianity has afflicted humanity, not only with erroneous doctrine, but with contention, bitterness, and carnage. Factious and ambitious men, "Schismaticks, Imposters, false Prophets, blind guides . . . set all in an uproar by their new doctrines . . . to the ruin and destruction of a Common-wealth" (3.385; see also 3.391). Burton draws examples from ecclesiastical history: Arians, Pelagians, Manichees, who in their day excited dissension and disruption (see further 3.419). Presumably he regards the Protestant extremists of his own England as similar trouble-makers. In religious wars and persecutions appalling slaughter is committed in the name of the Prince of Peace. "Because we are superstitious, irreligious . . . all these plagues and miseries come upon us; what can we look for else but mutual wars, slaughters, fearful ends in this life, and in the life to come eternal damnation?" (3.427). His examples tend to throw the guilt upon the Roman Catholics: the French Huguenot wars, the Spanish Inquisition, the wars in the Low Countries, England's *"Marian* times" (3.401, 432).

Such strife and persecution are wholly un-Christian: "We are all brethren in Christ, servants of one Lord, members of one body, and therefore are or should be at least dearly beloved, inseparably allied in the greatest bond of love and familiarity . . . as . . . in the primitive Church." But there is "No greater hate, more continuate, bitter faction, wars, persecution in all ages, than for matters of Religion" (3.399-400).

In his survey of the world that Christ died to save, Burton sets before his reader's eyes "a stupend, vast, infinite Ocean of incredible madness and folly" (3.359). If Democritus were alive, he would laugh at the "religious madness" of our age (1.56). To Democritus Junior, however, it is deeply disheartening to see mankind reject the comforts of "True Religion" for the agony attendant upon "Superstition." Other "grievances of body and mind, are troublesome for the time; but this is forever, eternal damnation" (3.398).

VII

Burton points an indignant finger at many villains who contribute to the miseries of mankind: the churlish aristocrat, the rich man who lives in ostentatious luxury, the self-seeking time-server, the cunning lawyer, the wily politician, the unscrupulous prelate—all those who serve their pride and their pleasure at the expense of others. Yet the ultimate blame, he realizes, cannot be laid upon scapegoats. It is human nature itself that is responsible for the human predicament.

What men suffer at the hands of other men, furthermore, is hardly comparable to what they inflict upon themselves. Our physical infirmities come of "our surfeiting, and drunkenness, our immoderate insatiable lust, and prodigious riot . . . Our intemperance it is that pulls so many several incurable diseases upon our heads, that hastens old age, perverts our temperature, and brings upon us sudden death" (1.156). Our wretchedness of spirit results from our misuse of our own God-given faculties. As a result of the Fall, we are "bad by nature," but we are "far worse by art, every man the greatest enemy unto himself. We study many times to undo ourselves, abusing those good things which God hath bestowed upon us, health, wealth, strength, wit, learning, art, memory, to our own destruction" (1.155).

Fundamentally man's unhappiness is due to his own failure in reasonable self-government, his surrender to his passions: "as long as we are ruled by reason, correct our inordinate appetite, and conform ourselves to God's word, [we] are as so many living saints: but if we give reins to lust, anger, ambition, pride . . . we degenerate into beasts, transform ourselves, overthrow our constitutions" and provoke an angry God to impose upon us "just and deserved punishment" (1.156).

The remedies for man's sinful miseries are very simple. The troubles of human society would vanish if each man simply followed the reasonable course of doing what his station and function obviously called upon him to do: "if Princes would do justice, Judges be upright, Clergymen truly devout, and so live as they teach, if great men would not be so insolent, if soldiers would quietly defend us . . . if Parents would be kind to their children, and they again obedient to their Parents . . . servants trusty to their Masters, Virgins chaste, Wives modest, Husbands would be loving. . . ." If individually we would "imitate *Christ* and his Apostles, live after God's laws, these mischiefs would not so frequently happen amongst us" (2.233). But though there are "many professed Christians," there are "few imitators of *Christ*" (1.56).

Burton is keenly conscious of the contrast between what humanity ought to be and what it is. He does not present the ideal with such clarity and emphasis as he might, yet there are frequent suggestions in the

Anatomy of what man should be and what he could be if he made sufficient effort of will. It is the ideal of the Christian humanist of the Renaissance. In spite of the Fall and of his consequent degeneration, man is still the noblest creature of God's world. He is lord of the earth, created in the image of God, or of "that immortal and incorporeal substance, with all the faculties and powers belonging unto it" (1.149). He is endowed with "reason, art, judgement" (1.155), with all the faculties requisite for knowing and loving God, for understanding and obeying his injunctions, for living a righteous and happy life, and for winning salvation hereafter. Man is a creature of highest potentiality and of most lamentable performance.

The basic cause of human tribulation is man's own slackness, his failure to follow the rule of reason and the will of God. The remedies for human troubles, individual and social, lie in man's own hands. By exercising the faculties which God has given, humanity could solve its problems. But mankind does not make the effort; it flounders miserably among troubles created by its own selfishness, savagery, pride, and frivolousness.

There is, however, more pity than condemnation in the *Anatomy*. The author extends his sympathy to many unfortunate categories of men: to the indigent laborer, "preyed upon . . . flead and fleeced" (1.406); to the "myriads of poor slaves, captives [who] work day and night in coal-pits, tin-mines" (2.151; *cf.* 1.397, 404); to prisoners in noisome dungeons "sequestered from all company but heart-eating melancholy" (1.398); to children who suffer from the tyrannies of severe parents and schoolmasters (1.322, 383-84); to his fellow scholars, harassed by poverty and humiliation. He understands the anguish of those who are mentally ill: the melancholy man tortured by griefs and fears for which there is no reason, the victim of the morbid conscience afflicted by a sense of sin and a doubt of salvation, the frustrated lover tormented by his longing, the husband who suffers the agony of groundless jealousy, even the pious fanatic who misleads others by his false doctrines. The mentally unbalanced are responsible neither for what they are nor for what they do.

It is presumptuous for any man to pass moral judgment on others. What shall become of men's souls "God alone can tell." Even to the suicide "His mercy may come . . . betwixt the bridge and the brook, the knife and the throat . . . Who knows how he may [have been] tempted? It is his case, it may be thine" (1.504-05).

VIII

In the *Anatomy* Burton does what he can toward the improvement of the human condition. For the correction of social evils, he proposes his utopia, his somewhat practical plan for a better social order. For men's mental ills, he prescribes pharmaceutical and dietary therapy of doubtful value and gives some very good advice on daily living ("*Be not solitary, be not idle,*" 3.494). Throughout the book he attacks the sin and folly of men with eloquent vituperation and brisk ridicule, seeking to do what may be done by the method of satire. Fundamentally, he is urging the exercise of reason. The recommendation of rational control is not at all novel, but it is possibly the best counsel that humanity has yet been offered.

Although, like others before him, Burton points out the ways of wisdom, he does not really believe that men will follow them. Men will persevere in their stubborn irrationality and will continue to suffer its consequences. "I was much moved," he says, "to see that abuse which I could not amend" (1.16). But though he cannot reform, he can console. To God's elect, the truly repentant, he offers the comforts of his predestinarian Christianity, and to tormented mankind in general he extends his understanding sympathy.

Burton has written a book abounding in gaiety, wit, humor, and satiric salt. The laughing philosopher nevertheless has presented a somber picture of the world. As he looks at human society, he sees strife and bloodshed, tyranny and insolence, greed and ostentation, chicanery and injustice, the prosperity of the stupid and evil, the poverty and frustration of the superior and deserving. When he looks at individual man, he sees a slave of passion who creates or enhances his own miseries. "*Aristotle* in his *Ethicks* holds *felix idemque sapiens*, to be wise and happy are reciprocal terms. *Bonus idemque sapiens honestus.* 'Tis *Tully's* paradox, *wise men are free, but fools are slaves*, liberty is a power to live according to [our] own laws, as we will ourselves. Who hath this liberty? Who is free? . . . where shall such a man be found? If no where, then *e diametro*, we are all slaves, senseless, or worse. *Nemo malus felix*. But no man is happy in this life, none good, therefore no man wise" (1.83-84). In this wretched world the miserable may hope ("SPERATE MISERI") but the fortunate should beware ("CAVETE FELICES," 3.494).

In composing *The Anatomy of Melancholy*, a scholar has drawn upon the accumulated wisdom of mankind to present a characterization and criticism of human nature and human experience. In spite of the title, the primary theme is the infelicity of man. The prevailing mood is compassion. The lasting interest and value of the book lie in its animated satiric representation of human life, in its perceptive explanations of life's harshness, and in the sympathetic counsel and consolation which the author extends to all whose burdens are too heavy.

BIBLIOGRAPHY

This is a selective bibliography of Burton material with a few very useful background items. It may be supplemented by the bibliography in Evans' *Psychiatry of Robert Burton* (1944). Information on the seventeenth century editions of the *Anatomy* and on reprints to 1930 appears in Jordan-Smith's *Bibliographia Burtoniana* (pp. 79-96).

The abbreviation *OBS* stands for *Oxford Bibliographical Society Proceedings and Papers*, vol. I (1922-26).

Bamborough, J. B., *The Little World of Man*, London, 1952.

Bensly, Edward, "Robert Burton, John Barclay and John Owen," *Cambridge History of English Literature*, IV (1910), 278-307.

—— "Some Alterations and Errors in Successive Editions of *The Anatomy of Melancholy*," *OBS*, pp. 198-215.

—— Numerous short pieces in *Notes and Queries*, 1903-09.

Browne, Robert M., "Robert Burton and the New Cosmology," *Modern Language Quarterly*, XIII (1952), 131-48.

Burton, Robert, *The Anatomy of Melancholy*, Ed. A. R. Shilleto, with an introduction by A. H. Bullen, London, 1926-27. (Originally published 1893.)

—— *The Anatomy of Melancholy*, Ed. Floyd Dell and Paul Jordan-Smith, New York, 1938. All-English edition. (Originally published 1927.)

—— *The Anatomy of Melancholy*, Ed. Holbrook Jackson, London, 1932 (Everyman's Library.)

—— *Robert Burton's Philosophaster with an English Translation of the Same. Together with His Other Minor Writings in Prose and Verse*, Trans. and ed. Paul Jordan-Smith, Stanford, Cal., 1931.

Bush, Douglas, Section on Burton in *English Literature in the Earlier Seventeenth Century: 1600-1660* (Oxford, 1945), pp. 280-86.

Craig, Hardin, Discussion of Burton in *The Enchanted Glass* (New York, 1936), pp. 238-51.

Duff, E. Gordon, "The Fifth Edition of Burton's *Anatomy of Melancholy*," *Library*, 4th series, IV (1923-24), pp. 81-101.

Escudero Ortuño, Alberto, *Concepto de la Melancolía en el Siglo XVII. Un Comentario a las Obras de Robert Burton y Alfonso de Santa Cruz*, Tesis, Huesca, Spain, 1950.

Evans, Bergen, *The Psychiatry of Robert Burton*, New York, 1944. In consultation with George J. Mohr, M. D.

Fox, Arthur W., "The Humorist: Robert Burton," *A Book of Bachelors* (Westminster, 1899), pp. 398-436.

Gibson, S., and F. R. D. Needham, "Lists of Burton's Library," *OBS*, pp. 222-46.

Gottlieb, Hans J., "Robert Burton's Knowledge of English Poetry," Unpublished dissertation, New York University, 1936.

Grace, William J., "Notes on Robert Burton and Milton," *Studies in Philology*, LII (1955), pp. 578-91.

Hallwachs, Robert G., "The Vogue of Robert Burton: 1798-1832," Unpublished master's thesis, Illinois, 1937.

—— "Additions and Revisions in the Second Edition of Burton's *Anatomy of Melancholy*: A Study of Burton's Chief Interests and of His Style as Shown in His Revisions," Unpublished dissertation, Princeton, 1942. Summarized in *Dissertation Abstracts*, XII (1952), 300-01. (Available on microfilm or Xerographic prints.)

Jackson, Holbrook, "Robert Burton His Book," *Book-Collector's Quarterly*, no. I (1930-31), pp. 9-22.

Kocher, Paul H., *Science and Religion in Elizabethan England*, San Marino, Cal., 1953.

Lievsay, John L., "Robert Burton's *De Consolatione*," *South Atlantic Quarterly*, LV (1956), pp. 329-36.

Lowes, John Livingston, "The Loveres Maladye of Hereos," *Modern Philology*, XI (1914), pp. 491-546.

Mueller, William R., *The Anatomy of Robert Burton's England*, Berkeley and Los Angeles, 1952.

—— "Robert Burton's Economic and Political Views," *Huntington Library Quarterly*, XI (1948), pp. 341-59.

—— "Robert Burton's Frontispiece," *Publications of the Modern Language Association*, LXIV (1949), pp. 1074-88.

—— "Robert Burton's 'Satyricall Preface,'" *Modern Language Quarterly*, XV (1954), pp. 28-35.

Murry, John Middleton, "Burton's 'Anatomy,'" *Countries of the Mind: Essays in Literary Criticism: First Series* (London, 1931), pp. 33-53.

Osler, Sir William, "Burton's Anatomy of Melancholy," *Yale Review*, new series, III (1913-14), pp. 251-71.

—— "Robert Burton: The Man, His Book, His Library," *OBS*, pp. 163-90.

—— "Extract from Creators, Transmuters, and Transmitters: Remarks made by Sir William Osler at the Opening of the Bodleian Shakespeare Tercentary Exhibition, April 24, 1916," *OBS*, pp. 216-18.

Patrick, J. Max, "Robert Burton's Utopianism," *Philological Quarterly*, XXVII (1948), pp. 345-58.

Pearson, Ellen M., "Burton's Utopia," Unpublished master's thesis, Columbia University, 1944.

Powys, Llewelyn, "Robert Burton," *Rats in the Sacristy* (London, 1937), pp. 185-95.

Prawer, Siegbert, "Burton's 'Anatomy of Melancholy,'" *Cambridge Journal*, I (1947-48), pp. 671-88.

BIBLIOGRAPHY

Putney, Rufus, " 'Our Vegetable Love': Marvell and Burton," *Studies in Honor of T. W. Baldwin*, Urbana, Ill., 1958), pp. 220-28.

Roberts, Kimberley S., and Norman P. Sacks, "Dom Duarte and Robert Burton: Two Men of Melancholy," *Journal of the History of Medicine and Allied Sciences*, IX (1954), pp. 21-37.

Jordan-Smith, Paul, *Bibliographia Burtoniana: A Study of Robert Burton's The Anatomy of Melancholy with a Bibliography of Burton's Writings*, Stanford, Cal., 1931.

────── *For the Love of Books: The Adventures of an Impecunious Collector*, New York, 1934.

────── "Footnote Smith," *American Book Collector*, vol. VII, no. 8 (April, 1957), pp. 3-7.

INDEX
(Selective)